# PRAISE FOR
## *Your Surefire Guide to CRM Success*

*"Bosma Enterprises employs nearly 130 people who are blind or visually impaired in a rapidly growing medical supply business. NexGen architected an end-to-end solution on the salesforce.com platform that not only helped us solve complex business problems, it is easily useable by people who are blind."*

**– HEATHER QUIGLEY-ALLEN, CFRE**

Vice President, Marketing and Resource Development

Executive Director, The Bosma Visionary Opportunities Foundation

*"NexGen's two-step process worked very well and allowed us to start using the application early in the process. This helped our management and end users become comfortable with the final solution. NexGen brought CRM best practice ideas to the table that helped us design a template that is allowing us to continue to meet our goals for the project. NexGen Consultants were extremely knowledgeable, helpful, and fully met all of our requirements and expectations throughout the entire project"*

**– BRYAN SCHATZMAN**

Chief Information Officer, Sun Chemical Corporation

*"NexGen was instrumental in assisting us with our Salesforce implementation on a very tight timeline. Their process of engagement and understanding of our needs allowed for a requirements and design phase with few iterations. The flexibility of their project team facilitated a quick turnaround on any requirement changes which allowed for a successful deployment."*

**– GREG HART**

Manager, IT Operations, Devicor Medical

T0145825

*"We had several requirements going into the project that NexGen was able to complete. They built a custom application, created a nightly data integration process with our Distribution Management systems and built tracking for our contracted and prospective agents and agencies. They understood our goals and built a solution that fit our business needs."*

**– MICHAEL C. VOGEL**
Vice President, Information Technology,
Ohio National Financial Services

*NexGen Consultants' development model offers a good value to the customer in terms of how they manage their resources to meet the development needs. NexGen's implementation and training approach enabled our team to become productive right away. Their ongoing support is responsive and collaborative."*

**– MARK BERMES**
Mutual Trust

*"NexGen has been a critical partner in developing custom solutions for us to effectively manage our business. Matt Mountain and Randy Davis have pushed Salesforce to its limits to meet our unique business needs for long-term Salesforce product adoption."*

**– PETER BURKE**
Vice President of Sales & Marketing, IBA Molecular North America, Inc.

*"As a non-profit, we were looking for efficient and cost-effective solutions to dramatically increasing our mission impact. NexGen created a scalable solution and helped us move to a paperless work-flow process resulting in a 3000% increase in our awards without adding staff."*

**– TODD SCHMIEDELER**
SVP, Employee Services & Foundation, Trilogy Health Services

*"I support over 600 partners, and NexGen is among the top of the partners who 'get it' and this book proves it."*

**– GREGG REID**

Alliances Director, Central Area – US, Salesforce.com

*"NexGen has been a very valuable partner on our Salesforce.com implementation. They have an excellent implementation process that is clearly defined and helps keep the implementation team on schedule and moving forward. They provided excellent leadership on our data conversion, and were quick to respond to our questions and changes. We used NexGen for our initial "Train the Trainer" training, allowing JTM System Administrators to train the users at large. NexGen also provided several management reports using Conga that allows us to track our R&D development projects as well as the Accounts, Contacts, and Opportunities being managed by our sales force. Overall, JTM Foodgroup and NexGen partnered on a Salesforce implementation project, and finished on schedule, and within budget. NexGen also provided post implementation support as needed to help insure that the Salesforce implementation was successful and providing JTM with our expected results."*

**– RAY LITTELMANN**

Business Process Manager, JTM Foodgroup

*""Nexgen is our integration partner of choice for our launch of salesforce. com in the US and Europe. They are extremely knowledgeable, keep their commitments, and very responsive when you are working toward time sensitive deadlines. The success of our global launch of salesforce.com is in part due to our partnership with Nexgen."*

**– AARON PENNELL**

Senior Manager Global Sales Effectiveness, Devicor Medical

*"Our company needed a focused, highly effective Salesforce.com implementation team to convert and improve upon our existing CRM footprint. We found that and more in NexGen. Within a few weeks, we were training our sales and customer support teams on Salesforce.com and the more efficient processes we adopted as part of the transition. In the years since, we've happily asked NexGen to return for CRM best practices review and training."*

**– MIKE MCGRATH**

Vice President of Information Technology, American Commercial Lines

*"NexGen did such a fantastic job of implementing SalesForce through our entire sales team, within a year, we realized it was the product that could help many other departments within our organization and installed it there as well. The customizations they were able to facilitate allowed us to continue to run our business with the processes we already had in place. Having the entire company working from one CRM solution has been invaluable to our growth!"*

**– GREG EHEMANN**

VP Sales, Shoptech Software

*"I have been working with NexGen since 2011 with multiple financial advisors all over the United States. Their ability to provide custom CRM solutions has enabled the companies I work with to expand and grow their respective businesses at an incredible rate. My experience with this company has been nothing less than stellar and I would personally recommend them with my highest rating! You owe it to your business to check them out and see for yourself how good they are."*

**– MARK GAFFNEY**

Director of Marketing, Strategic Wealth Designers

*"Roto-Rooter looked very diligently for the absolute best partner to assist with integration of Salesforce.com to our sales teams. Matt & Randy (NexGen) brought the absolute best approach to understanding our business, our culture and the schedule in driving a rock-solid solution. We trusted the right partner to get the implementation done the first time. I couldn't be happier with our choice!"*

**– PAUL NAGLICH**

Director, IT Services Group

*"Our experience with NexGen Consultants was outstanding. Their team made the difference…hands on, highly responsive, and knowledgeable. They took the time to understand our business needs, and completed the project on schedule. NexGen has a great combination of knowledge and business acumen that makes them an excellent integration provider."*

**– MIKE KERSEY**

Manager, Application Design and Development, Cardinal Health, Specialty Solutions

# YOUR SUREFIRE GUIDE TO
# CRM SUCCESS

MATT MOUNTAIN & RANDY DAVIS

# YOUR **SUREFIRE GUIDE** TO
# CRM SUCCESS

NO MORE LEAVING **MONEY** ON THE TABLE

Published by Advantage, Charleston, South Carolina.
Member of Advantage Media Group.

ADVANTAGE is a registered trademark and the Advantage colophon is a trademark of Advantage Media Group, Inc.

Printed in the United States of America.

ISBN: 978-1-59932-537-8
LCCN: 2015933122

Book design by Megan Elger.

This publication is designed to provide accurate and authoritative information in regard to the subject matter covered. It is sold with the understanding that the publisher is not engaged in rendering legal, accounting, or other professional services. If legal advice or other expert assistance is required, the services of a competent professional person should be sought.

Advantage Media Group is proud to be a part of the Tree Neutral® program. Tree Neutral offsets the number of trees consumed in the production and printing of this book by taking proactive steps such as planting trees in direct proportion to the number of trees used to print books. To learn more about Tree Neutral, please visit www.treeneutral.com. To learn more about Advantage's commitment to being a responsible steward of the environment, please visit www.advantagefamily.com/green

Advantage Media Group is a publisher of business, self-improvement, and professional development books and online learning. We help entrepreneurs, business leaders, and professionals share their Stories, Passion, and Knowledge to help others Learn & Grow. Do you have a manuscript or book idea that you would like us to consider for publishing? Please visit advantagefamily.com or call 1.866.775.1696.

*Dedicated to the NexGen Consultants' team for their tireless commitment to establishing NexGen as one of the highest rated Salesforce.com partners for customer satisfaction.*

# CONTENTS

A 2014 study from Nucleus Research found that companies get, on average, an impressive $8.71 return for every dollar they spend on Customer Relationship Management (CRM) software. At the same time, a 2013 study from Forrester Research found that 70 percent of all CRM projects fail to deliver the expected results. These are general statistics spanning businesses both large and small, in all kinds of industries. So what's going on here? How can some companies be getting so much out of CRM while others are branded as "failures"?

Over the past seven years, we have overseen CRM implementations for hundreds and hundreds of businesses, so we are in a position to understand firsthand why some companies succeed and others "fail." Now, failure can mean a lot of different things in this context. As defined by the Forrester study, it means the project didn't deliver expected results (which means it may still have led to a return on investment). Perhaps the project was over budget or didn't meet the intended business objective. Or perhaps the project, once complete, just died on the vine, meaning after implementation, company employees simply didn't use the software—we've heard of *many* examples of that kind of scenario over the years, and Forrester Research cites a lack of user adoption as the primary cause of failure. Whatever the reason, we do know two things for sure: that the failure rate of CRM is much higher than most people would expect and that the potential for a return on their investment is *much* higher as well.

---

## A BIG RETURN ON CRM INVESTMENT

A 2014 study from Nucleus Research found that companies get $8.71 return for every dollar they spend on CRM software. That's up from $5.60 in 2011.

---

## WHY DO SO MANY COMPANIES FAIL WHILE OTHERS SUCCEED?

In many cases, the reason why companies fail to meet their businesses objectives when it comes to implementing a new CRM system is because of the way they defined those objectives in the first place. Misconceptions about what CRM can do leads to expectations that doom people to failure before they can even get started. In other cases, the rush to get a CRM project completed leads to a lack of alignment across the organization. No one has taken the time to get everyone on the same page and to buy into the same goal, so what senior management wants ends up being something vastly different than what the sales reps, or the main users of the software, want. Finally, when it comes to business objectives, a scenario that we see all too often is companies that have no real business objective at all. They think they need a CRM solution because all of their partners and competitors have one. "I need it because Joe has it," is the kind of thing we hear all the time. But when it comes to setting goals and to figuring out what they want CRM to do for their particular business, they haven't a clue.

We witnessed this kind of situation when we worked with a large healthcare organization. They made it all the way through the implementation process without having any goals at all for the outcome. Not surprisingly, when they first started using their new CRM tools, they had trouble because they were using the tools without a purpose. There was significant data duplication (i.e., multiple contact records for a single contact), no consistent definition for users about what the data they were entering and using should mean, and no clearly defined sales process built into the CRM that sales reps could follow. As a result, adoption was very low. It was like driving in unknown territory without a road map or even a destination. It doesn't really matter whether you are in a Ferrari or an old beat-up Chevy, if you don't have a road map, you are going to get lost and probably end up driving aimlessly all over the place. And if you don't have a destination, how are you going to know when you've arrived where you want to be?

Thankfully, this organization didn't just continue driving around aimlessly forever. They realized their mistake and took steps to remedy it. They made the investment of bringing in an expert to help them get their act together around their sales processes. Then they got leadership involved by designating a smart and well-respected IT executive to sponsor the project and drive adoption within the organization. With the right resources and sponsorship in place, they were able to gain a very clear vision of what they wanted to gain. Now, they're using the software much more effectively than they ever were before.

## WHY THIS BOOK?

Failures, unfortunately, are far too common when it comes to CRM. We, and everyone else in this business, see them all the time. In fact, we've seen a whole parking lot full of them and have come to understand that there are very clear and distinct patterns as to why it happens. Our intent with this book is to eliminate those failures. We know from experience that it doesn't have to be this way.

In addition, we want to do more than just help you avoid failure; we want to show you how you have enormous success. When it comes to CRM software, we know that the average return on investment for successful implementations is $8.71 per $1 spent. That's a pretty great return, and when that number is revealed to people, it typically elicits oohs and aahs. But our message is that we want you to top that. And you can. With the right information, perspective, and a little bit of work, you can get a remarkable return.

We want you to use this book to ask the right questions and give you the crucial information you need to define your CRM goals and then to get everyone aligned around them. If you can get everyone to buy into a vision, your chance of success is going to be significantly higher. Management must know what sales wants, and sales must know what management wants, so everyone can work together toward success.

Our job is to manage the successful implementation of CRM software in businesses large and small, across a wide range of industries. But by the time we come into the picture, most of the businesses we work with have already decided to do the project. They have hired us to execute, not to ask questions like, "Do you have a clear vision for why you want this?" or, "Does everyone in your organization understand that vision and believe in it?" We do our best to get alignment and push our clients on these points, but in a sense, we come to the party a little too late. The big decisions have already been made. What this book will do is help you educate yourself about the wide range of possibilities when it comes to CRM solutions and help you set the right goals for your organization, so that when you are ready to call a partner like us to help you with your CRM implementation, you're starting off on the right foot for success.

It may sound obvious that organizations need goals and alignment for the success of any project, not just a CRM project. Though it may sound obvious, it unfortunately isn't common practice. Companies routinely spend anywhere from $10,000 to $50,000 a year on CRM or more—often a lot more—without ever stopping to ask themselves the critical questions: Why do we need this? What are our goals for it? What does success look like? Are we aligned, within our organization, on those goals and benchmarks for success? And that's a big reason why there is so much failure. Companies are not getting a return on their investment because they haven't spent the time up front to define these things and get buy-in from everybody involved.

## WHAT EXACTLY IS CRM, AND WHY DO YOU NEED TO THINK SERIOUSLY ABOUT IT?

When clients come to us, a lot of them don't fully understand what CRM is and what it can do. CRM stands for Customer Relationship Management, but that doesn't really define it. In fact, that can mean very different things to different people, and many people think CRM isn't much more than an extension of the sales team's contact list. It can be a whole lot more than that, however. And it can be about a lot more than just sales. For example, some organizations, like Amazon, take orders online versus traditional direct sales methods. Although they don't have a traditional sales model, they effectively use CRM concepts to take their prospects through a personalized shopping experience. Other companies use their CRM systems across multiple departments, including marketing, operations, and customer service. The possibilities are a lot broader than most people realize.

One of the reasons why people don't take the time to fully understand what CRM is and what it can do is that it's a relatively cheap investment to make, one that's within reach of most companies, even small businesses. Compared to an Enterprise Resource Planning (ERP) system, which companies spend millions of dollars to implement, investments in CRM are proportionally less. That puts a lot less pressure on people to justify their decision. But that doesn't mean it's a good idea to invest even a modest amount in something you don't understand or when you don't know what you're going to get out of it. Even if you may not be losing a lot on your initial investment if it doesn't work out, why lose anything at all if you don't have to? What's more, think about all the money you could be leaving on the table. If your competitors are getting more than 800% of return on every dollar they invested in their CRM, then don't you want to get at least that much too?

So what is CRM? It could broadly be defined as people, processes, and technology that interface with customers. What you really want to focus on most is the interactions between these three things. The problem is that most people out there don't view it that way. They see CRM as just a technology, and that really limits their understanding of what it can do for their business. And if they don't fully understand the possibilities, they are almost surely leaving money on the table.

Most CRM platforms are designed to be highly configurable. CRM can and should be tailored to the specific needs and goals of your business. That's why it's not just a piece of technology that you buy and install. You have to have the human participation and processes around it to make it really work for your business.

We take a broad view of CRM, one that includes an expanded definition of the word "customer." As you will come to understand in the coming pages, CRM can encompass the entire sales process, so the relationships you can manage go well beyond just your typical customer or the person who buys the good or services you are selling. You can also use the tools to manage your relationships with partners, distributors, and even different departments within your organization.

As you read through this book and contemplate CRM solutions in the context of your own business, you should focus on the broad definition we've stated here, not the narrow one of technology. It will not only enhance your understanding of CRM, it will open your mind and help you see what's possible.

## A WORKING DEFINITION OF CRM

For us and for the purposes of this book, we define CRM as the interactions among people, processes, and technology that interface with customers.

## ABOUT US

We've been working as Salesforce partners for the past seven years, but that's just one part of our total CRM experience. Prior to that, Matt used the CRM system, Gold Mine, for thirteen years. Randy too has used a number of CRM platforms at various companies over the course of twenty-five years. We have been in the sales trenches and used these systems ourselves before we moved on to the company we have now, which manages CRM implementations. So we've had a chance to experience the potential and the problems of CRM from multiple perspectives.

As members of sales teams at various companies, we saw what it was like to be told by executives that we had to use a new CRM system. A lot of times, our colleagues on the sales team hated these systems. And it's no wonder why. How often were members of the sales team involved in helping to evaluate the CRM system prior to implementation? How often were they, as the primary users of the system, asked to give input on what they needed and what would make their jobs easier? Almost never.

When Matt and I started using Salesforce.com more than seven years ago, it was by far the best CRM solution that we had ever encountered. That was back in 2007, and Matt got the idea to see if there were any Salesforce.com partners in our area. There were none, so we looked at each other and said, "Hey, it's early. We can have the advantage of being the first mover in the Cincinnati area (where we're located) and in the Midwest in general. Let's do it." That's how NexGen Consulting was born.

Since that time we've worked on more than 700 projects for businesses and organizations across the U.S. and even internationally. Those companies have come from a wide range of industries, from healthcare to financial services to manufacturing and many more. We are one of the highest rated implementation partners for Salesforce from a customer satisfaction standpoint. A year ago, we started placing a huge emphasis on user adoption. We weave user adoption ideas into the equation to help make sure people *want* to use the new system. Sometimes management will have to spend a little bit more money to help drive user adoption, but it's a great way to distinguish themselves from the competition because a lot of companies—most companies in fact—don't do this.

Here is the important thing to understand: Anybody can implement CRM. You can load it, add a few fields, and then turn to your sales team and say, "Look what we've got! Go use it." But that alone isn't likely to work. As we've mentioned, with CRM, there is a huge potential for success, but there is also a rather alarming rate of failure. And even though you can get by with investing just a few thousand dollars to get CRM up and running, even that is a big price tag for something that's just going to sit in your systems and not be used.

Our goal with this book is to make sure that that isn't you, that yours isn't the business that implements CRM and then, several years down the road, discovers that no one is using it. Or even that people aren't using it to its full potential. We want to set you up for not just success but wild success, for a big return on your investment. This book is your first step on that journey.

## HOW TO USE THIS BOOK

To give you a full picture of CRM and all its challenges and possibilities, we broke up this book into three parts that mirror the three basic stages of integrating CRM into your business. We have done this because at each of these three stages, there are different things to understand and consider to maximize your potential for success.

The three stages are:

- Part I: Intention—In this section, we'll talk about how to think through your reasons for wanting CRM and what it can do for you.

- Part II: Implementation—This covers the process of implementing a CRM system into your business, including the best approach to take to ensure widespread adoption and that you meet your goals.

- Part III: Follow Through—CRM is not something you implement and then you're done. This section talks about how to set yourself up so that you continue to have success with your CRM system over the long term.

We encourage you to read through the entire book before you start your own CRM project. Take it stage by stage, and think through each before jumping in. Despite the high rates of failure, this process doesn't have to be difficult. You can make this work regardless of whether your company is big or small, whether the investment you make is large or modest. The key is to have a plan that suits your business's unique needs. And this book will help do just that!

# PART I

# INTENTION

This section covers how companies typically think about CRM, what their usual reasons (both good and bad) are for wanting to implement a system, and how well they understand what CRM can and can't do to improve their business. Together, these chapters will help you gain perspective and formulate a plan that makes sense for your business. In fact, formulating a plan is something you can and probably should do before you even start looking into products.

# CHAPTER 1

# THE WRONG REASONS

This first stage, the intentions stage, where you think through your reasons for wanting a CRM system and what you plan to get out of it, is the one where companies most often fall short. The reason is that many of them don't take the time to do it right. The result is that many companies launch into a CRM project for the wrong reasons. By wrong reasons, we mean ones that will set them up either to fail or to not get as much out of the final result as they could.

We could go on for pages and pages about all the many wrong reasons why people want CRM software. In this chapter, we will cover just the most common. We do this to help you learn from others' mistakes and avoid some of the most common pitfalls. As we discuss each "wrong reason," we'll also talk about how that reason led to inferior results. And then, in the next chapter, we'll look at the other side of the coin—the right reasons—so you can begin to see how you can best set yourself up for CRM success.

## "MANAGEMENT WANTS TO PLAY BIG BROTHER"

The number one, most common wrong reason we see is that executives want to better monitor their sales reps. To put it bluntly, coming in with that kind of reasoning will simply kill the project.

A lot of managers are probably thinking, "But that's my job. I'm supposed to be monitoring my employees." Of course you are, but the fundamental problem with this kind of intention is that sales reps won't see the win for them personally in giving executives more information. And sales reps are, in most companies, the primary users of CRM. If they're not motivated, they won't use it. Simple as that. Or they will do the bare minimum they need to do to make their bosses happy, instead of using the tool to make any real improvements in the way they do business.

Here's the fundamental issue. Salespeople, on average, are more social and outgoing; they're not likely to be introverts. That's why they're salespeople. More often than not, they are not what we would call left-brained folks as compared to an operations person who doesn't mind organizing and documenting data and paying a lot of attention to detail. They are more about getting out and talking to people, making connections, and having interactions. Oftentimes, they don't want to be accountable to anybody in terms of what they do in their day-to-day. "Hey look, I make my number every year, so leave me alone," is a typical response. Or, "What do you care if I play golf four days a week if I'm making my quota. Now you want to change the way I work? Screw that." To ask anyone to change the way they do business without showing them the win for them personally is very difficult. To ask someone who likes to spend his time outside the office interacting with people to spend more time tied to his computer is difficult. A system is only as good as its users. So if your primary users aren't using it or they're annoyed about using it or they're not using it to its full potential, then you're not going to get a very good result.

We see it happen all the time: Management makes a decision to install a CRM system so they can better monitor the pipeline, so they can see who is doing what and make judgments based on that information. A typical response from a sales rep might be: "Why should I spend my time filling out my pipeline when it takes away from my selling time? How is filling out a pipeline report going to help me sell more business? And isn't that my job?" At the end of the day, those are legitimate questions too. A sales rep's benchmark is usually pretty simple. "Am I making more money?" If he isn't making more money, he doesn't care. A lot of organizations don't realize what it's going to take to motivate their sales reps and make them happy, which is all about showing them how CRM can be a win for them, too. Don't underestimate what it's going to take to do that or you could be one of those businesses where, six months down the road, the CRM system is installed but it's barely being used—if at all.

Now, if you have a CRM system with an ability to intake leads, do some kind of lead scoring and then produce a report about the most-qualified leads that a sales rep can focus on. Now you have something to offer your salesperson. Or, if you can set up the system so that it automatically sends a notice to the boss when approval is needed on a price without the rep having to stop what he's doing and make a call—maybe multiple calls, if he can't get his boss on the phone—that's something that will have real appeal to most sales reps who would love to spend less time doing that kind of administrative stuff, which takes away from their selling time. Making someone's job easier and cutting down on their busywork is a real upside that you can sell to your sales reps.

Of course, if sales reps are motivated to use CRM software as part of the way they do their daily business, then management will end up getting the insight they are looking for. But you can't go into this thinking only about what management wants, because management alone won't make it successful. Everyone who uses CRM must be able to get something out of it, and they must understand that value up front to drive adoption. Coming across like you want the sales team to do a bunch of extra work just so it's easier for you to play Big Brother is not going to get you what you're looking for. We said it before, but we'll say it again, because it's crucial: The system is only as good as its users, so those users better be a big part of your primary reason for implementing a new CRM system in the first place.

## "MANAGEMENT WANTS A BETTER PICTURE OF THE KPIs"

Most executives love key performance indicators, KPIs. They tend to be the kind of people who love to look at the dashboards that can be built into a CRM system to assess the health of the pipeline, to help with forecasts, and to monitor things like close ratios or the average number of calls it takes a rep to win a sale or the average number of calls per week that a sales rep makes. Lots of people get enamored by all the data they can access when they are first exposed to a CRM system. But keep in mind that those dashboards are only as good as the data they display. If the data is wrong, outdated, or missing entirely, then what good does it do you to see it nicely displayed in a dashboard?

Like the point before, this comes back to your primary user, the person who will be entering that data and keeping it up to date, which is usually your sales rep. You have to think about why a sales rep would want to spend his time entering data to produce those KPI reports that management is so interested in seeing. Does it help him make more sales? Does it help make his job easier? Because, unless it helps him do his job, he's not going to care.

Suppose you call a meeting of your sales team tomorrow to tell everyone that they have to start keeping all this data about each of their clients up to date. What are they going to think? Their first reaction will probably be that it's just going to take time away from the customers, time away from doing what they need to do to make sales. So why should they do it? What often happens as a result is that some sales reps just throw numbers into the system to make it look like they have been listening to you. Other sales reps might even ignore you and do nothing at all. And how useful are those dashboards going to be if they're based on unreliable data entered by unwilling sales reps?

If you're going to require the users to spend one extra minute to enter data, then you had better be saving them a minute down the road. That's part of getting buy-in. Now, there are all sorts of ways to make this idea more appealing for the sales rep. For example, if you are willing to spend, say, $10,000 for an admin who can enter data for the reps, someone who is available to take a call from a sales rep while he's on the road and say, "Oh sure, I can update your pipeline for you, just tell me the info." Now you're onto something. Now your sales rep cares. He's got the support he needs, and he doesn't have to stop what he's doing to type in data for you. Or maybe you build a speech-to-text tool into your system so it's easier for your rep to enter information on the fly. Doing so doesn't slow him or her down. If the task you are assigning your sales reps is hard or time-consuming and they don't see any upside for them personally, then it's probably not going to get done. And you're simply not going to end up with good, reliable data for your KPIs.

There's a phrase we've been hearing for years, which is: "If it's not in Salesforce.com, it didn't happen." We hate that phrase, because guess what? The fact that it's not in Salesforce doesn't mean it didn't happen. It did happen. It still counts. You may not know about it, but it happened. If you're using CRM to monitor your KPIs, you have to be honest about what sort of picture it's giving you. It could very well be a misleading picture or an incomplete picture of what's really happening. And to get a complete picture, you have to have the main providers of that data you want (again, typically your sales reps) fully on board.

## "WE WANT TO FIX THE CULTURE PROBLEM IN OUR SALES DEPARTMENT"

A lot of times, managers want CRM to solve a problem that CRM just can't solve on its own. Maybe their sales reps have bad attitudes or they aren't documenting their work. It's fascinating how often people think that if they buy their sales reps a brand spanking new CRM, it will change their behavior.

Here are some of the cultural problems that we've seen managers try to use CRM to fix: The sales department functions like a collection of individuals instead of a team. Management wants there to be more sharing of information among the sales reps. Management wants the sales reps to collaborate more with each other and with other departments, like marketing and operations. Management wants sales reps to do more cross-selling and upselling. Those are all good end results, but simply implementing a new software system isn't going to fix these things on its own.

CRM can give organizations the ability to collaborate much more easily and effectively, especially across multiple departments and territories, where people don't get a chance to work together in person. But remember the broad definition of CRM, which we spelled out in the introduction. It's about the interaction among the people, processes, and technology that interface with customers. So the technology is just one component of it. Sometimes people implement a system hoping it will fulfill their goal of bringing more cohesiveness to their organization. CRM can be an invaluable tool for enhancing cohesiveness, but it can't do it on its own. You also have to think about bringing team members along so they share that goal and giving them the processes they need to accomplish it.

## "WE WANT TO FIX THE PROCESS PROBLEMS IN OUR SALES DEPARTMENT"

CRM is great for streamlining or automating processes. Suppose you're a sales rep who occasionally forgets to make follow-up calls. The system can put those calls on your calendar and automatically prompt you when the time comes, so, without a lot of effort on your part, you never (or almost never) forget again. Or suppose you sent out a proposal to a customer, and you're wondering if she has looked at it yet. CRM can show you whether an email has been opened without you having to make a call and bother the customer.

There are tons of things that CRM can do to improve your processes, but like we said about cultural problems, CRM is only part of the solution. It gives you the tools you need to have highly effective and efficient processes, but if your current processes are screwed up, CRM can't fix them on its own. What we often see instead is that the implementation of a new CRM system brings to light process problems that were previously unseen or ignored. A common example of this is companies that don't have any rules and processes around the data they collect. Maybe different sales reps keep different kinds of data depending on what they think is most useful. Or maybe some don't keep much data at all. When a CRM system is implemented, it can become obvious pretty quickly if your data is not reliable.

To give you an example, we once worked with a company where the CFO sponsored their CRM implementation. The reason the CFO did it was because he wanted the sales team to do a better job of collecting data so that he could access that data to create all kinds of different reports (those KPIs again). Well, this was mostly an older sales force that wasn't used to collecting or keeping up the kind of data he wanted. So, after the CRM was implemented, he looked with great excitement and saw that there was practically no data at all populated in the system. Rather than take that information and look at ways to offer the sales force the motivation and processes they might need to get the job done, he got upset. He was so upset that he issued a report showing all the data each sales person was missing and giving them each a score as to how badly they had failed. It was essentially a public reprimand, and guess what? It didn't work. That tactic did nothing to solve the problem they had, which was that there were no processes in place to make data collection feasible or reliable. So the sales reps simply didn't care if the CFO wanted more data.

## "I WANT TO MODERNIZE MY SALES FORCE."

Maybe you don't have a very tech-savvy sales force. Maybe many of your reps are older, and they like the way they have been doing things for the past several decades. But suppose that most of your sales force is going to retire within five years, and when they walk out the door, you don't want all their contacts and knowledge to walk out the door with them. You want to capture that information, which makes good business sense. But this is a problem that CRM alone can't solve.

Again, this comes back to how you present the change to your sales reps and how you make it worth their time to use the new program. With a sales force that isn't tech savvy, the burden may be even greater. Not only do you have to make it worth their while to use the new CRM software, you also have to make it appealing to learn to use technology in the first place. With some people, it's just not as intuitive as it may be with a younger workforce who grew up with laptops and smartphones attached to their hips. If you try to force the issue, it can be like pushing water uphill. Your sales reps may just say, "Screw you. I'm out of here." And then all that knowledge goes out with them.

In other words, technology is not going to make your sales team tech savvy. This may be a case where you have to introduce the system in layers, starting out with just the basics to capture contacts and the like and then gradually build sophistication as people learn or as less tech-savvy reps retire and new ones come in. CRM is flexible enough to do this if you know what your priorities are.

This might also be a situation where you really need to budget for some support for your sales team. Reps might not be willing to keep up all their contacts on their own, but if they have access to an admin, someone whose job—either entirely or in part—is about helping the sales rep use CRM effectively, that can make the idea a whole lot more appealing. And if you know up front that that's something you will need, then you can plan for it and budget for it, and it can be part of how you introduce the new system to the team.

## "BECAUSE MY COMPETITORS HAVE IT" OR WORSE ... FOR NO KNOWN REASON AT ALL

We hear this one all the time. "My competitors have CRM, so we should have it too." Or, "I keep hearing about how important this CRM thing is, so we need it in our business." Well, why? For what purpose? What do you want it to do for you?

We talked earlier about how doing something without a reason or end goal is like getting in your car without a destination. You will end up just driving around aimlessly. And yet, this is the reason that *many* businesses have for implementing CRM. If this is you, it's important to stop and spend some time educating yourself and thinking through the possibilities before you just plow ahead. It's hard to gain a return on your investment if you haven't spent any time thinking about what that return ought to be. And you might just end up throwing money down the drain. As we've mentioned, we have seen many companies over the years spend their money and effort to implement a CRM system, only to see it sitting there unused months or years down the line. Spend some time setting yourself up for success (more on this in the next chapter), so you don't become one of the negative statistics.

## "I'M GOING TO BRING IN CRM TO MAKE MY SALES TEAM MORE PRODUCTIVE"

This is not a bad reason really, but we include it here among the "wrong reasons" because it may be a sign that you're missing out on a lot of the opportunities that CRM can bring. The opportunity to integrate marketing efforts, for example, or to coordinate better with operations are things you may be missing out on if you limit your thinking to just how CRM can help your sales department.

You may very well start off by implementing just for sales, but it's important to have a holistic view of what you want CRM to do for your organization overall before you get started. In the end, it may be that a basic automation is what works best for your business. But for others, just looking at the basics and only considering what CRM can do for sales may mean you are leaving money on the table. You could do more if you contemplate a more holistic and long-term view. And if you're going to dedicate your time and resources to implementing this new system, don't you want to get as much out of it as you can? We like to say, "Think broadly and implement incrementally." (We'll talk more about thinking broadly in chapter four.)

## A FINAL WORD ON WRONG REASONS

What is the problem with people having the wrong reasons? To put it bluntly, they might as well give us half of what they were going to spend on the project and walk away. Because either the company's ROI could be higher because they're missing out on opportunities, or they are going to fail entirely. It's not only a waste of money, but it also wastes the time of everyone involved. It can also negatively impact the company culture and damage morale, particularly if employees feel like they are being jerked around or overburdened or like they are being watched because they aren't trusted by management to do their jobs.

CRM projects are often highly visible across an organization. And it's not like being a manufacturer and buying a new piece of equipment that fails. CRM is not only visible internally, but it's often also visible to the customer. You have to calculate the failure exponentially, because it can have a big ripple effect. Not only is there a financial cost, but there are also potential costs in damaging the trust of your employees and confusing your customers if processes or customer-facing systems change and then change again. If you look at it this way, the cost can be exponential compared to other investments.

The person who is managing the CRM project has his job on the line, too, because failing on a highly visible project can be a real black mark against someone. But it doesn't have to be. Success is not hard to come by if you just have the right information and perspective. With that in mind, let's now look at some of the "right reasons" for launching a new CRM project in your business.

## CRM DON'TS

Set yourself up for success by avoiding the following traps:

- Don't expect your team to get excited about your new CRM system if what you want most is to play Big Brother and look over the shoulders of your team members.

- Don't expect your team to get excited about your new CRM if what you want most is to get a better picture of your KPIs.

- Don't expect CRM alone to fix culture problems within your sales department.

- Don't expect CRM alone to fix process problems within your sales department.

- Don't expect CRM alone to modernize a less than tech-savvy sales force.

- Don't expect to be successful with CRM if you haven't thought through your reasons for wanting it in the first place.

# CHAPTER 2

# THE RIGHT REASONS

Who can benefit from CRM? The short answer is—practically any company in any industry today has the potential to benefit from CRM.

Some companies can benefit from CRM more than they even realize. For example, organizations that could benefit from increased collaboration, where team selling is involved, where cross-communication is essential, where information sharing is essential, can get a lot out of a CRM system. Another example is organizations that need to manage an entire customer life cycle, and many companies do. There are very few companies today that simply sell you pencils and then they're done. Even pencil sellers want to come back and sell you more office supplies and make you into a repeat customer. Organizations that are managing a longer customer life cycle, from customer acquisition to taking the customer through the sales process to managing postsale issues to cross-sell and upsell, can get a lot out of CRM, too. Those situations require lots of collaboration and lots of information sharing, which the system can facilitate, and the value of CRM grows exponentially compared to a business that doesn't focus on a full customer life cycle.

Some companies may not even realize they can benefit from CRM. When people think about CRM, the first thing that comes to mind is sales, which isn't necessarily accurate. There are a lot of organizations where companies don't sell, people just buy, but a CRM system could still be extremely valuable because ERP systems aren't flexible enough to handle their data. An online retailer, such as Amazon, is a good example, where Amazon is not out selling to the customer; customers come to them through Amazon offering a simple and personalized shopping experience.

When CRM fails, it typically isn't because it wasn't right for the company. As we said, practically any company has the potential to benefit from CRM today. The difference between success and failure is less a question of *if* CRM is a good idea and more a question of whether or not companies approach it in the right way. And that starts with doing it for the *right reasons*.

We talked through some of the most common wrong reasons in the last chapter to help you steer clear of the pitfalls. Now let's look at some of the positive reasons for embarking on a CRM project, which will set you up for success.

## BECAUSE IT WILL BENEFIT THE USER

By "user," we mean the sales reps and other employees who will be the main users of your CRM system. In the last chapter, we tried to drive home the idea that any system is only as good as its users. If they don't understand how CRM benefits them, then they simply won't use it to its full potential. Or worse, they may not use it at all. In this section, we will detail some of the most common ways that people can benefit from using CRM in their daily work routine. These are things that make their jobs easier and give them more time to do what they like to do best, which is interact with clients. One of the most important things to remember from a management perspective is that you need to make sure these benefits are clear from the very beginning in order to get buy-in from your users.

### Enhanced Efficiency

A CRM system's ability to streamline processes and automate tasks can offer huge payback to its users. It can help them stay on top of things and cut down on the amount of time it takes them to do the kind of busywork or administrative tasks that are part of everyone's job. That frees up time for sales reps to focus on what they like to do best, which is selling.

There are lots of ways to gain efficiencies through the use of CRM. One tool that works well for a lot of sales reps is a speech-to-text tool, which gives them the ability to dictate notes right into the system. When a rep walks out of a meeting, if he doesn't record his notes right away, he is likely to forget. A lot of us are guilty of this. We don't take the time to record what happens with clients because we're too busy running to our next meeting. But that can cost us even more time in the long run as we try to recreate those notes at a later date, as well as negatively impact our relationship with clients if we forget crucial information. Being able to dictate your notes on the fly, have them translated to text, and then stored in CRM, where they are centralized, can be a big help. It means you don't have to worry about doing it when you get back to the office and the memories have faded or even when you get home at night exhausted from a long day. That can be a huge benefit, especially for people on the road.

The centralization of information is also a big benefit. It's much easier and faster to find what you need when you need it because everything is stored in one place. In our business, for example, every single signed contract is put into our CRM system under the client record, so we always know exactly where to find it. That way, we don't have to spend a lot of time searching for files when we are getting ready to talk to a client.

For sales people who are dealing with a lot of clients, CRM can help them track whether or not they have made a proposal available to a prospect, if the prospect has opened it, and how many times the proposal has been viewed. You don't get that kind of visibility if you just send something by email. Then, CRM can prompt you to follow-up on that proposal at the right time. Features like these help keep you organized and in better touch with your clients with less effort on your part.

These are just a few of the many ways that CRM can stream-line a user's workday. What's most important is to make sure that the efficiency-enhancing features you choose are the ones that are going to be most useful and appealing to your main users.

## More Time and Mental Energy

Let's say that you need to stay in touch with your A clients more than your B clients and your B clients more than your C clients. Just keeping track of all that can be time consuming and confusing, especially if you have a particularly long client list. But if the system could do that for you and automatically notify you when it's time to set up your next appointment, wouldn't that be beneficial? It means you don't have to have your own system for keeping track of all that information, and you're much less likely to lose track of things or forget important meetings.

Along the same lines, perhaps there are steps you have to go through to get sign-off on a contract and close a deal. Maybe legal needs to look at it or your boss needs to approve the quote. Rather than making several phone calls to get in touch with these people and then following up with them to make sure they have done what you need them to do, CRM can do all that for you. It can automatically send out emails to the right people, prompt them if they don't respond in a certain amount of time, and then notify you when the approvals come through. Without you doing a thing.

These days, we are all doing more work than people have ever done in the past. The new business model is that we just have to work faster and smarter. Having a system that can do some of your work for you, by recording data or automatically sending out requests or setting up tasks, can really make your life less hectic and more organized. And less time and energy spent organizing oneself, hunting down information, or doing routine tasks means more time available to generate leads and close deals. Making that clear to users will significantly help drive adoption.

### Providing Additional Information

When you pull up a client record in CRM, wouldn't it be great if, right there on the page, you could see if there was any new news about the company, something you might want to know about before you meet with them? A news report about a new product launch or an acquisition or even layoffs, for example. And, wouldn't it be great to know who else from your company has talked to them recently and what they talked about before you walk into a meeting? That way, you're not retreading old ground or contradicting your colleagues. And, wouldn't it be good to know before you meet with a client if they have had or are currently having any issues with your company? If they have a history of back payments or they are angry that their last shipment came in late, if would be very useful to know that before walking into a room with them. All that can be documented in CRM, so you can review the information and be prepared before you meet with a client. And being well informed about a client can have a huge impact on how effective your interactions with them are.

In many companies, when a sales rep walks out the door, a lot of that kind of information walks out with them. Then the new rep starts with a blank slate, even though the client may have all kinds of past history with the company and all sorts of expectations that the new rep isn't aware of. If that information is recorded and made accessible, then when you come into a new territory, you can read up on it. You are not calling on clients and asking them the same stupid questions that someone has already asked them in the past.

## UNDERSTANDING WHAT WILL BENEFIT YOUR MAIN USERS

All sales reps are not the same, and what will benefit one team may not be the same as what will benefit another. You have to have a good understanding of how your reps operate on a daily basis in order to understand how CRM can benefit them most. Following are some questions to ask to give you the kind of insight you need:

- Are your salespeople road warriors?

- If they are, are they mostly traveling by car or by plane? Are they spending a lot of time sitting in airports?

- Are your sales reps paid by commission or salary?

- Are they dealing mostly with existing clients and repeat business, or are they mostly hunting down new leads?

- Do reps generate their own proposals and quotes, or do they get help with the configuration or pricing?

- Is it important to keep a knowledge base of your competitors that can be updated and accessed by every person to share knowledge about their pricing, sales tactics, etc.?

- Does you company respond to many RFI/RFPs (Request for Information/Request for Proposals) and if so, how much time do you spend, on average, responding to them?

- Would there be value in providing a graphic representation in CRM that shows sales trends by client?

The answers to these questions can have a significant impact on how you design your CRM system. To give just one example, there's nothing more frustrating to a sales rep than not being able to make a quick note on his smartphone while he's in an airport waiting on a plane. If he has to pull out his laptop, make sure it's charged, and boot it up just to enter his notes, that can be a huge hassle. What's worse, he may not even have time for all that, which means the note is left unrecorded. For someone who travels a lot, being able to access CRM from his phone or tablet is practically essential.

## THE RIGHT PERSPECTIVE FOR MANAGEMENT

In the first half of this chapter, we talked about how one of the most important "right reasons" for implementing CRM has to be because it benefits your users. That means a shift in perspective for many executives, who sometimes approach a new CRM project by thinking only about what they want out of the system, which is a good way to alienate your main users. In this section, we'll talk about some more ways that management can ensure they are embarking on this project with the right perspective, one that will set them and their whole team up for success.

### You Are Willing to Do What It Takes to Make the System Work for *Your* Business

There is not a one-size-fits-all CRM solution for businesses. The companies who think there is are often the ones that fail and are no longer using the system six months down the road. What's good for one customer may not be good for another. Managers who understand that and then take the time to figure out what will work best for them—meaning for both management and the users—before jumping into the implementation stage are the ones that typically succeed.

### You Have a Strong Executive Sponsor

Is it important that you have a sponsor for your new CRM project and that the sponsor is somebody who is familiar with sales, if that's who your main users will be. There's no better sponsor than an ex-salesperson who has been elevated to a senior sales management role but still has a great relationship with the salespeople. A person like that has been in the sale staff's shoes and understands what they do on a daily basis. They are familiar with what sales reps need to sell and can ensure that the system is being created to meet the needs of their main users. This is also a person who generally has a lot of credibility among the sales staff, which goes a long way toward driving adoption.

In our experience, the CFO is often not an ideal sponsor. CFOs typically get caught up in all the data they will be able to access and the dashboards that can display their KPIs. But as we pointed out in the last chapter, those dashboards are only as good as the data they display, which may or may not be accurate and reliable. So if that's your main reason for launching a new CRM, you're likely setting yourself up to fail.

### You Have Thought About How CRM Can Positively Impact Your Customer

One reason that CRMs fail is because people only look at them in terms of the impact they are going to have internally and don't think about the customer. If your company's goal is to get a higher score on customer satisfaction or on being easy to do business with, you have to look at whether your CRM system is set up to support those goals. Take e-signature, for example. If you build an e-signature feature into your CRM, then customers don't have to print off a contract, sign it, and fax it back. It's a lot easier for the customer to sign a contract electronically.

It's also a benefit to the customer if the sales rep calling on them has a broad view of their account. What incidents have occurred? What are the recent quotes? What are the recent orders? A lot of companies build their CRM with a focus on the reporting pipeline but not on this level of customer information. That can have a real impact on your customer. For example, say a sales rep has closed a contract that says the customer can buy so many tons of steel at a certain rate. Well, whenever that customer buys steel, he doesn't call the sales rep; he calls operations and places his order, and those contacts may not show up in CRM. A few months later, the sales rep might sit down with the customer to renew his contract, only to be surprised to find out that the customer is ticked off. "I had to send back five tons of steel today because what you guys sent me was all wrong," he might say. Because the sales rep isn't involved in fulfilling orders, he would likely have no idea that there have been problems, and his lack of awareness could make the customer even angrier.

This kind of situation is very common in the sales world. Sales reps, who often have the closest relationship with the customer, can get completely blindsided because they aren't aware of a major issue. You have to think about how the choices you make when implementing CRM are going to affect your customer.

**You Are Ready to Align Management Methods with CRM**

It's amazing how many companies make the investment in CRM and then continue doing business the same way they always did. But smart managers see the implementation of a new CRM system as an opportunity to use the tools the system offers to streamline their own management processes and to look at what is working and what could work better.

We had a big customer that did a fabulous job of exactly that. They dropped all their old methods for doing pipeline reviews. Instead, they said, "We're going to use CRM for our pipeline reviews. We're going to have a consistent method for how we define our pipeline. We're going to have a consistent meaning for our pipeline stages. And everybody is going to understand those in order to facilitate communication." Then they jettisoned their traditional way of conducting pipeline meetings, where they all got on a conference call and talked about their pipeline and instead had Web meetings where everyone got into the CRM system and looked at the pipelines together as they talked.

This group used CRM to drive process improvements, which really helped get everyone on the same page. The reps liked it because there was no longer any ambiguity about what something meant. If an opportunity was in the qualified stage, for example, everyone understood exactly what "qualified" meant. It had been unclear before, but now there were clear criteria around what terms were supposed to mean.

## COMPANYWIDE BENEFITS

We have tried to drive the point home that walking into a new CRM project with only ideas about how it is going to benefit management is a recipe for failure. But that doesn't mean that management can't also make good on many of their own reasons for wanting CRM, as long as they have the right perspective and are focused on their users first. It's all about how you approach the project and what your priorities are. Following is a discussion of some of the common reasons why management often wants CRM, which are well within their reach if they go about this the right way.

### Capture Information That's Essential to Your Business

It's a common problem that information, which has only been recorded in the salesperson's head or personal notes, walks out the door with them when they move on to their next job or retire. It's important for any business to capture contacts and information so that when your sales reps leave—and in many industries, there's high turnover in such positions these days—there isn't a lot of disruption to the business. We talked before about how that's not a good enough reason to motivate your sales force to use the system, but if you've given them plenty of motivation in other ways, then they will happily input the information you want to capture, which can really benefit the company as a whole by helping to maintain good working relationships with customers even as sales reps come and go.

### Appeal to a Younger, More Tech-Savvy Workforce

Talent can be very hard to come by in business today. A lot of people, especially younger workers, expect to be able to use technology to help them do their jobs. They're used to having their phone attached to their hip and expect it to be a tool they can use on a daily business. In fact, a company that expects them to work in an old-fashioned, paper-based system might put off younger workers.

As we've tried to say in a number of different ways, before designing your CRM, you have to ask yourself how your sales reps like to work. Part of that answer depends on how tech savvy they are. For businesses with a lot of younger workers, it can be worth making a bigger investment in CRM so that the system is accessible with smartphones and tablets and there is a better user experience that's tailored to those devices, because that's not only what will motivate their employees to use the system, it's also what they expect from living in a technologically advanced world. That's how many people like to work today, and that can be really important when you're trying to attract new talent.

We have a customer that attracts a lot of young sales talent. We did a CRM implementation for them, and when we went back a month or two later, the young people on their staff had figured out ways to use it that we hadn't shown them. In some cases, they were doing things that we didn't even know were possible, like integrating their data with Google Maps to help them come up with more efficient routes for their sales calls. We didn't tell them how to do that. They did it on their own because that's the way they like to work.

**Enhance Collaboration within Your Business**

This is a big one for a lot of managers. Today, so much collaboration is done around calls, email, chats, and all that gets lost. If you had a system where all your collaborations around prospects, customers, and things you were doing to make the business better could be done and recorded in one system, that could enhance collaboration across all groups, not just sales.

Consider the idea of workflow management. Companies spend hundreds of thousands of dollars on workflow management tools that can streamline their processes, but that's just another system. If you're not careful, pretty soon you could have all these different systems that people have to learn and use. But if you could have one system where all your operational and sales processes can be managed in one place, there is a huge benefit there in terms of making things easier and more streamlined for your employees and saving money by not paying for multiple systems. Many companies never consider that idea, because they think CRM is just for sales. The idea of using it across groups is something they just haven't wrapped their heads around, even though it could be hugely beneficial to have more collaboration between various departments, like marketing, operations, fulfillment, customer service, and sales, rather than having each department work separately and on separate systems.

For example, think about how a better system of collaboration could enhance your customer service. A customer calls and says, "Hey, this product doesn't work." They might be calling the sales rep, because that's who their main contact is, but that sales rep doesn't know how to fix the problem. So the sales rep needs to engage the engineering team. If that issue is tracked and centralized, you might be able to spot trends among customers who are reporting similar issues. But if it's all done by email correspondence, you might never see the common threads.

Another example involves service agreements. A customer buys a product or service and with that, they get a four-hour response time during the week and an eight-hour response time on weekends. Well, when a call comes in, who's watching the clock? Wouldn't it be helpful if there was an automatic escalation at three hours, signaling people, "Hey, nobody has followed up on this." That would make it easier for people to collaborate and get something resolved.

The possibilities are endless when it comes to encouraging collaboration, but to give just one more example, we work with a manufacturer that struggled with coordinating between sales and operations. Oftentimes, when a sales person gets in touch with a prospect, that prospect will want samples. The company's process for such situations was for the sales person to make a phone call or fill out a piece of paper and fax it to another department to get samples sent out. The problem was, not only was that a pain for the sales rep, but it also wasn't a very reliable process. Oftentimes, the sales rep had to follow up one or more times to make sure the samples actually got sent. The groups weren't working together very efficiently at all. But, if the sales rep had the ability to pull up the customer and request a sample through the CRM, the system could automatically prompt operations to fill that order and notify the sales person when the sample went out. That would help the two departments work together more effectively and efficiently. Just as importantly, it would lead to more satisfied customers who got what they asked for in a timely manner.

## 5 QUESTIONS TO MAKE SURE YOUR REASONS ARE THE RIGHT REASONS

If you embark on your CRM project with the right reasons and perspective, you will have set yourself up to get the best results. Here are some questions to ask yourself to make sure you're in the right frame of mind:

- Are you focused on how CRM will benefit your main user?

- Are you willing to do what it takes to make the system work for the specific needs of *your* business?

- Do you have a strong executive sponsor?

- Have you thought about how CRM can positively impact your customer?

- Are you ready to align your management methods with CRM?

# CHAPTER 3

# RETURN ON INVESTMENT

When we first heard the results of the Nucleus Research, which found that successful CRM implementations enjoy, on average, an $8.71 return for every $1 they spend on the software, we were at a conference, and the crowd was audibly impressed. It is an impressive number, but it may not be the best way to think about your own return on investment when you're just embarking on a CRM project. Very few companies we work with say, "Because I'm putting this much in, I'm going to let two people go and therefore save X amount of dollars." Typically, companies aren't going to significantly reduce costs by implementing a new CRM system. What they are really trying to do is make their people and their processes more efficient, so that they can grow without adding staff.

By the same token, very few companies say, "Because we're implementing this system, our sales reps are going to be able to close four more deals a year." That may very well be what happens in the end, because CRM should make the sales rep's job easier and more efficient, giving him more time to sell and close deals. But that is not the kind of ROI that most companies are willing to commit to up front. Most would have a hard time saying that they are going to be able to raise reps' quotas by a half million dollars annually because they now have this tool.

That doesn't mean it isn't important to have a clear picture from the outset of the ROI that you want to get from CRM. This is another way of thinking about goals. You should be asking yourself: What do I want to get out of this in the end, and are the decisions I'm making supporting that end? In this chapter, we will walk you through what kind of ROI you can expect, so that you have a better vision for where you want to end up.

## SOFT VS. HARD BENEFITS

An $8.71 return on a $1 investment is definitely a hard benefit, but it's not the *only* kind of return you can expect from CRM. A useful way to think about this is to consider both the hard and soft benefits. For example, if you could streamline the process for getting samples to customers, what are the benefits? What's the ROI on that? Well, the customer will be happier, and that's important. That kind of soft benefit may be hard to calculate, but everyone knows that having happy customers is crucial to any business.

At the same time, you may be able to calculate some hard numbers around that process improvement. Say you now only spend one hour getting a sample filled and shipped as opposed to the three hours it took before. That saves you two hours per sample. How many samples do you send out? Say it's about one per day, which means you're saving about two hours each day or about a quarter of a person. And what's the average salary? Maybe it's $40,000, so your savings is $10,000. But are you really saving $10,000? No, because you're not going to fire a quarter of a person. But there is a benefit there. Someone now has two hours more each day to work on something else, which can grow your business.

Sometimes you also have to think about preventing a negative ROI rather than creating a positive one. For example, capturing contacts so that you're not losing information due to employee turnover is a negative ROI that's certainly worth preventing. But again, it would be hard to calculate a dollar amount to attach to that kind of benefit.

What you really need to consider here in terms of ROI is two things: what the savings and benefits are and what the savings and benefits are that will be reflected in your bottom line. Those are two different things. You can gain a lot of efficiencies with CRM, but they won't be reflected in your bottom line immediately. They won't show up until down the road, when the efficiency you've gained and the losses you've prevented allow you to grow at a faster pace.

Soft benefits, however, can be hard for companies to picture, especially if they are contemplating investing in CRM for the first time. The sections that follow will explain some of the common benefits you can expect so you can start to picture how CRM can improve your business.

## IMPROVING PROCESSES AND STRATEGIES

Here is something we hear a lot from businesses that are thinking about implementing CRM: "We want it so we can figure out what changes we need to make to improve our business. Because right now, we don't have the information we need to make good decisions." CRM can help. For example, CRM can help you see where you should be focusing your marketing dollars. A lot of companies have no idea what kind of return on investment they're getting on their marketing campaigns, but CRM can track the results of a campaign and show efforts turned into sales. Then you have a basis for a real ROI.

## PINPOINTING SUCCESSFUL BEHAVIORS AND STRATEGIES

Another problem we hear a lot of from companies is: "I don't know which activities lead to success in my salespeople." That's a problem that CRM can certainly help businesses with. With a CRM, you can find out what kinds of activities successful salespeople are doing. You can find out if there is a pattern. You can track, for example, whether there is a correlation between the number of corporate visits a salesperson performs and the rate of success or between a certain kind of customer presentation and the rate of success or between having certain sales engineers on calls and the rate of success. Without CRM to track that kind of data to analyze, you may not have any idea how to determine which factors lead to success. If you have the information, then you can figure out what adjustments to make in order to get better at what you do and drive more sales.

This can be a great return, but it also harkens back to something we talked about in chapter one when we discussed the wrong reasons. If all management wants to do is play Big Brother, then this ROI isn't going to work for them. You need sales reps on board so that they are accurately and routinely entering the data that management needs to make those decisions. That means introducing CRM in a positive way, as something that's going to help reps improve their performance, make more sales, and make their jobs easier, rather than something that's going to help management catch employees in the act of doing something wrong.

## IMPROVING EMPLOYEE FEEDBACK

Related to the above is the idea that more insight into how employees work and which behaviors produce the best results can make managers better at managing. This kind of insight can help you know how to guide people and develop their skills. Because if you don't really know what someone is doing, it's difficult to provide useful feedback. And if you don't really know what works, it's even more difficult. But if you have the right information, you can offer people personalized feedback tailored to them. And practically everyone appreciates being treated as an individual.

## INFORMATION SHARING

Another big ROI is information sharing. One of the top comments we get from our customers is that managers don't know what their sales reps are doing and sales reps don't know what other sales reps are doing, even when they're calling on the same accounts. That is usually because they don't have the means to share. Sales reps have their heads down. They're running hard to make quota. If they come up with a new sales method or a great new PowerPoint that illustrates their product or service in a better way, maybe they'll send out an email sharing that development. Maybe. But there's often no collective process around sharing that kind of information or tools.

Think about something as simple as sharing contacts. Suppose I've got all of my contacts in Outlook, Joe's got all of his contacts in Outlook, and our manager has all his contacts in Outlook. Then I get a new mobile number from one of my clients, which I update in my Outlook contacts. I now have the latest contact info for that clients, but nobody else knows what that customer's new mobile number is. And that's just one small piece of information. Imagine that multiplied across all the bits and pieces of information that each person in your company gets every day. A lot of sales reps keep quite a bit of information on their contacts, including the customer's anniversary, spouse's name, kids' names, where the customer went to school, and so on. None of that gets shared in Outlook, even if there are other reps that call on the same customer. And when that sales rep leaves, all that information is gone. And that's just one small example of how not sharing information can impact a business. If people are not sharing contacts, then they are almost surely *not* sharing any information about more effective sales practices either.

## BUILDING ON PRIOR KNOWLEDGE

Sales people often work very much on their own and not as a team, but think about how beneficial it might be if they pooled some of their resources. For example, say a sales rep has put together a proposal in Excel and Word. Then, next week, another sales rep needs to put together another proposal, which is very similar to what the first rep just did. But that rep has to start from scratch because he doesn't even know about the proposal the first rep did, and there is no way to search through everybody's brain to see if they've done one of these before. If proposals were centralized, then that person could search and say, "Oh, yeah, we just did one of those. Let me see what their proposal looks like and use that as a starting point." That makes a lot more sense than having everyone start from the beginning each and every time.

CRM can take that idea even further, making it even easier to capitalize on work that's already been done. When companies respond to RFPs, for example, oftentimes there are a lot of standard questions that show up again and again. Imagine a feature where CRM could read the question and auto-populate the answers based on previous RFPs, so that people don't have to manually type in the answers again and again. That can be a great way to build on prior knowledge as well as a huge time-saver. There is huge ROI there.

## GETTING EMPLOYEES UP TO SPEED MORE QUICKLY

A lot of companies spend significant resources on getting new employees trained and up to speed. Anything that can make that process quicker and more effective can result in big ROI for a business. Think about call centers, for example. The ramp-up for getting a call center to provide great service to clients is huge. What if you could centralize all of the approved answers to common questions in order to give customer service representatives a knowledge base to start with. Then, instead of having to wait until they've gone through four weeks of training, a new rep can be up to speed in a week, because the tool provides a lot of basic knowledge at their fingertips. There's real ROI there for call centers in particular because they typically go through people quickly. Anything you can do to get new employees up to speed faster and more efficiently provides real benefits to the organization.

## INSIGHT INTO QUOTING

A lot of companies have guidelines and policies around discounting, but when reps send actual quotes to customers, management might have no idea how much they are actually discounting. In addition, many companies have no idea what the win rates are based on different levels of discounts. Think about the ROI you could get if you built a quoting function into your CRM so that you could track how many quotes went out, how many were offered a certain discount level, and how many were won or lost at each level. That would give you great insight into pricing. A company might end up saying, "Well, for this product, we probably ought to lower the standard price, because we're never getting the standard price" Or, "We're seeing a discount threshold of 25 percent all the time, and we're still pretty darn profitable at a 25 percent discount. We ought to send out a notice to our team, saying, 'Hey, let's go with a standard 25 percent discount for this product for the next six months and see what happens.'" It's surprising how often management lacks real insight into quoting and which quotes really work for the customer. But when they have the insight, the payoff can be huge.

## COLLABORATING WITH PARTNERS

The benefits of CRM aren't limited to tracking interactions with your end customer. CRM can give you a picture of your entire sales process and how it works. A lot of companies, for example, sell through distribution partners, and a lot of valuable information and insight can be lost because of a lack of direct access to the customers. Companies in this situation can give their partners access to their CRM system so partners can use it to place orders, share leads, log clients issues to get the manufacturer's help, and so on. That means more efficient processes as well as more information sharing with the partner.

## A FEW WORDS OF CAUTION ABOUT ROI

Once people start to understand how much insight CRM can give them into how their business is working, they can sometimes go overboard. Burdening sales reps with too much detail around account planning and territory planning is a pitfall that we see companies fall into far too often. You have to ask yourself, "Is this really going to add value to the rep?" Otherwise, why are you asking them to spend their time on it? Sure, you want to know about customer trends, industry trends, and what's going on in each territory, but you always need to balance your desire for more insight and knowledge against the burden you are placing on your sales reps or other main users. Otherwise, they might come to resent the new system and all they're being asked to do as a result of it. One of the biggest benefits of CRM is the opportunity to do work more efficiently, but if you're causing a lot of busywork for your reps because they have all these different categories of information that they have to fill out, then those efficiency gains can quickly go right out the window.

Randy recalls, when he was a sales rep, selling software and services for various companies that required reps to develop overly detailed account plans. But he never saw any value as a result. It never seemed to lead to more sales, more activity, more anything. Besides that, filling them out led to guesswork because reps were being asked questions such as what the customer's sales run rate was going to be over the next two years. (In many cases, the customers themselves couldn't predict this with much accuracy!) As a result, most reps just made stuff up that had no basis in reality just so they could fill in their plans. And they resented management for taking up their time with useless tasks when they could have been doing something else.

It's also important not to confuse adoption with a positive ROI. Here's what we see happening too often: It comes down from on high that sales reps are supposed to make ten calls a week. Well, guess what? All of a sudden, reps are logging ten calls per week whether they make them or not. Or reps are told that they are expected to be logged into the system for a certain number of hours each week. Well, people don't want to be called out by their managers or end up on the login "wall of shame," so they log in every day. That may get people to use the system, but by itself, it does not give you a great return on your investment. In a sense, adoption has to be looked at separately from ROI, because there is a difference between getting people to do what you ask them to do and getting them to be effective at what they do. Just because you have evidence that people are using CRM doesn't mean they are using it well.

## A FINAL THOUGHT ON ROI

Another way to look at your return on investment is to consider what the ROI is on putting in a new manufacturing or financial software system. I can guarantee it isn't positive. But you know you can't run a business without these things. We use QuickBooks for example. We must have it, so we pay for it, but it would be hard to calculate the ROI we get from QuickBooks in terms of dollars and cents.

That doesn't mean it isn't important to understand your goals for getting a new system or the soft ROI that you expect from it. If you focus on those things first, then everything else will fall into place. How are you going to justify spending X number of dollars on this system? You may end up saying something like, "In Phase I, there is going to be a negative ROI. It may cost us, but we have to do it." But that's fine, because in Phase 2, you are really going to start seeing the benefits.

It's important to have that kind of long-term vision of what the payoff is going to be. A lot of companies approach partners like us asking for bids on a CRM implementation. Because they haven't defined their goals and because they don't know what kind of return they are looking for, they have nothing to go on when comparing quotes except for the price. But the cheapest price isn't necessarily going to set you up to get the return you want. It may not allow you to have the insight into employee practices or partner activities that you're looking for. It may not allow you to coordinate with departments beyond just sales. People under-invest in CRM all the time because there is almost always a way to get it cheaper. To which we have to say, "Great, if sales aren't that important to you, then do it as cheaply as you can, because I would too."

# PART II

# IMPLEMENTATION

This section covers the process of implementing CRM in an existing business. In it, we will talk about where to start, what you need to be thinking about, and the right approach to take to help ensure widespread adoption, along with some industry best practices for both implementation and training.

# CHAPTER 4

# THINK BROADLY

Once you have thought through your intentions or reasons for wanting to embark on a CRM project and have decided to move forward, the question becomes, "Where do we start?" The advice we like to give is this: Think broadly and then implement incrementally.

It all starts with a vision. In the last section, we outlined many of the things that CRMs don't fix, like bad business processes, sales reps with negative attitudes, or a dysfunctional culture. To understand what CRM *can do* for you, you want to start by thinking broadly and considering the full range of opportunities that you can capitalize on.

You also want to think about your corporate goals. What are they, and how will CRM align with those goals? This is about getting corporate alignment. (Then you take a bottom-up approach to meet those goals, which we will cover in the next chapter.)

In this chapter, we'll show you how to think broadly about CRM so you can kick off your implementation with a goal-focused vision and a full understanding of what CRM can do for you. This is how you can make sure that you aren't overlooking opportunities or leaving money on the table.

## A BROAD VIEW OF "WHEN?"

It happens all the time. Companies launch a new CRM project without much forethought and without any real goals or ROI in mind. As a result, they start off in the wrong place.

A common scenario is this: Somebody at the executive level says, "We're going to implement a CRM, and I want it done by the end of the year." All of the sudden, the focus goes to timeframe. That is, quite simply, a counterproductive, culture-killing way to frame your objective. It has no rhyme or reason to it. It is just an arbitrary deadline, detached from any real business purpose or justification.

Instead of setting a deadline as your first decision pertaining to the project, focus on creating energy and enthusiasm. We're not saying that it's a bad idea to have a soft timeline objective, but don't put the cart before the horse. There is a lot to consider and figure out before determining what sort of timeline is appropriate for the scope of your project. We sometimes see a project team panicking because they're scared they're going to miss their deadline. Then they hit their deadline, and all hell breaks loose because the details of their implementation were not thought through very well to begin with. The CRM is not what people want, it doesn't meet corporate goals, and no one is happy as a result.

It simply doesn't make sense to worry about how long a project will take *before* you think about how CRM is going to function within your business and what you want the end result to be. Since CRM can and should be tailored to your business, the implementation process may be very different for one company vs. another. A smaller business may opt for a basic implementation, while a larger national organization with a diverse sales force may want to include a lot more features and functions. The timeline for those two projects would be very different because the scopes are very different. There are times when a company has a legacy CRM and the licensing is going to run out by a certain date, which puts time pressure on the project right off the bat, but that's the exception to the rule. In most cases, the deadlines that are set are arbitrary, just some date on the calendar that someone in authority chose. So why start there?

When setting a deadline for your project, ask yourself: "Why this date?" If there's no compelling answer, then it's a "phantom date," as we like to call it. You are better off starting with a "what" or a "how" question like, "What do I want CRM to do for my business?" or, "How is this implementation going to affect my team?" This is not to say that deadlines aren't important. No one wants an implementation to drag on and on and never finish. The main point is that the question of when is not the most effective starting place for most businesses.

A better approach would be one where an executive sponsor creates enthusiasm and energy within the business, especially among the people who are going to be the main users of CRM and then determines a soft timeline around a pilot. One executive sponsor that we worked with reinforced this approach very effectively in the way he ran progress meetings. Instead of asking at the outset of each project meeting whether we were on track to meet our deadline, his first questions always were: "Are we making progress? What are the issues? How are we going to tackle them?" At some point in the process, he had gained enough insight into what his company's goals were for CRM and what it would take to reach them to set a real deadline, but it was a date based on knowledge and common sense. It was part of a broader vision of how the CRM was going to be constructed and how it would support the sales team, rather than having an executive say something like, "I want this done before my performance review." That kind of deadline may make management look good, but it's not taking into account what's best for your primary users, which, as we talked about in the last section, is a not the best way to set yourself up for success.

## A BROAD VIEW OF THE POSSIBILITIES

Many people think CRM is just for salespeople and all it can do is track their pipelines and manage their contacts. But there are so many more things that CRM can do. To give just a few examples, CRM can create a proposal for you. It can track how well you're doing compared to your quota. It can be used to record all the customer service issues that a client has had, so you know what his experience has been with your company before you talk to him. It can be used to warm up prospects before you even call on them so you're maximizing your in-person time. It can be used to cut down on the number of manual activities you need to do by letting the system do some of them for you.

There are so many things CRM can do, but if you go into the process thinking you just want to track customer phone numbers, customer interactions, and any open opportunities you have with them, you may be missing out. That is a pretty basic usage of a CRM system, and you may be missing opportunities to improve your business that you don't even know about yet.

Another drawback to that way of thinking is that you aren't going to find too many sales reps who are excited about signing up to use that kind of basic CRM system. You will just be requiring more work of them without a lot of payoff for them personally. That doesn't mean you can't start off with a simple implementation, one which just covers the basics, and expand from there, but if that's the route you choose, it should be an informed decision based on a long-term view of your goals.

To make sure you're thinking broadly enough, the first step is to educate yourself about what CRM can do. If you understand the possibilities, you can then choose what works best for your business and your budget.

## BENEFITS OF THE BROAD VIEW

Starting off with a broad view of the possibilities allows you to do several beneficial things:

1. Get a fuller picture of what your needs are and think through the different ways CRM can help you. The broader the vision, the higher the potential ROI.

2. Get people excited about the possibilities from the outset, so that when the time comes, they *want* to use the system rather than feeling like it's a chore or just another thing on their to-do lists.

3. Define your priorities so a realistic, objective-based timeline can be created for your implementation of what should be done first and what will come next.

## PUT YOUR CUSTOMER IN THE CENTER

Another way to take a broad view is to start off by thinking not just about your sales reps and how they will use the system but also about your customer. Put your customer in the center and think about how CRM might ultimately benefit your customer relationships. If you understand the experience your customer has with your company and areas in which that experience might improve, then you can align the capabilities of CRM to improve that experience. This goes back to what we said in the last section about CRM not just being about sales reps. In the end, it's your customers that you want to make happy.

Thinking about CRM from the outside in, rather than the other way around, can help you better understand all the different ways the system can impact your customer. Use the questions in the sidebar to help you do this. For example, the first question is: "Are we hard or easy to do business with?" A lot of organizations don't realize that engaging your customers through technology today is pretty darn simple. A big area of CRM growth is called a "community," which is about setting up communities for your customers so they can collaborate not only with you but also with each other about ideas for new products, ideas for product improvements, and troubleshooting issues. Using CRM to improve customer engagement is an opportunity that a lot of companies miss.

Another way to look at this is to consider how all the different people and departments within your business interact with the customer. Ask yourself: "Does everybody in the organization know what's going on with the customer?" In our experience, one of the top reasons why people want a CRM system is because the right hand doesn't know what the left hand is doing. For example, suppose a customer just submitted a high-priority ticket because they are really unhappy about something. That information doesn't get back to the sales rep, who then walks into a meeting with that customer to ask for more business. He doesn't have a clue that the customer is upset with his company's service, which is obviously not going to make the customer feel like his concerns are being taken care of. And it's probably not the best time for the sales rep to be asking for more business. CRM can help you centralize information about the customer so everyone can access it, and information like that can really help enhance your customer interactions.

## AM I CUSTOMER FOCUSED?

To help you think through how CRM can help enhance your customer relationships, start by asking yourself the following questions:

- Is my organization hard to do business with because my clients can't make inquiries or get information off our website?

- Does it appear to my clients that there is a lack of communication and organization among various groups in our company?

- Do I make it harder than it should be for my clients to sign off on proposals?

- Am I collaborating with my clients at all times (during the presale process and after the sale)?

- If they can't find knowledge to solve their problems, do customers have to call the customer service department, where they get put on hold for too long?

- Do I treat my worst customers with the same level of service as my best customers? After all, it can be hard to distinguish who my best customers are. Many people consider their best customers to be the ones who spend the most money; however, what if we looked at gross profit by customer and determined how we treat clients based on that metric instead?

## THINK BROADLY ABOUT THE CUSTOMER LIFE CYCLE

CRM stands for Customer Relationship Management, but the reach into other areas of business often goes untapped. CRM doesn't have to be just about managing customers through the sales cycle. There are likely opportunities for using CRM to improve your business throughout the entire customer life cycle, from mass marketing and prospecting to customer service and repeat business. Picture the entire life cycle and then ask yourself: Where are our gaps? Where are we falling behind? What could we do to improve our customer interactions? What could we do to attract more customers?

As we said before, despite taking this kind of broad view, you may still start off with a simple implementation, one that focuses on quoting, for example. However, it's important to build your system with a view to how you're going to grow it and address more areas of your business over the long term. That has an effect both on design and on getting buy-in from the people in your organization. That's why it's so important to take this kind of broad view *before* you give someone a prescription for implementing your CRM system.

For example, we see organizations all the time that spend tens of thousands of dollars on marketing campaigns and then don't have any idea if their reps are following up on the leads the campaign generated. That's because they're thinking only about one aspect of the campaign and not about what the follow-through is going to be on it. Picturing, or even mapping out, your customer life cycle, starting with marketing and taking it all the way through account management and customer service, can be an enlightening exercise for a lot of companies. It can show you things like how many people within your organization are touching the customer, which groups have no idea what other groups are doing, or where processes, like ones for following up on marketing leads or updating data, are falling short. It can start to reveal not just inefficiencies but also where the biggest opportunities are for growth.

Following are some more examples of how picturing your entire life cycle and all the different people and departments involved in that cycle can help you find more ways in which CRM can improve your business.

### Accounting

Suppose that when a sales rep gets a new prospect, he needs to engage accounting and have a credit check done. Why not have the system request that check from accounting automatically? And then have accounting record in CRM when the check is done so that the rep knows if he's okay to proceed with this potential client or shouldn't waste his time. Wouldn't most sales reps love to have that kind of routine task taken off their plates rather than having to remember to call accounting to make the request and then call them again to follow-up?

## Operations

The reach CRM can have into operations is often hugely untapped. One of the largest implementations we've ever done encompassed operations, and the company designated a tagline of "process improvement" for the project. Not only does their system serve as a CRM, but it's also driving operational improvements across sales, operations, and customer service, all of which leads to happier customers and potentially lower costs.

## Shipping

Shipping can be an area that has a big impact on the customer. Suppose a customer places an order and, for whatever reason, fulfillment is late. It's incredibly helpful for a salesperson to know that when they are interacting with a client. If that kind of information is centralized in CRM, then the rep will not get blindsided by walking unaware into a meeting with an unhappy client.

## Legal

Even looping the legal department into your CRM system can benefit some companies. If your business tends to have a lot of revisions to agreements, for example, then that back-and-forth can be done through CRM, so the process is recorded and efficient. It's an easy way for sales reps to involve legal without a lot of effort on their part.

## Engineering

Some organizations have a lot of engineering or technical people who get involved in the sales process to explain or help engineer the solution. We have seen tremendous strides made by manufacturing companies that have used CRM to enable these groups to work together more efficiently, which has reduced their overall cost of sale. There can be better coordination between sales reps and experts through CRM.

### Account Management

Salespeople are the hunters, while account managers are the farmers. Account managers take existing clients and sell them more. Even within sales departments, you have hunters and farmers, and they may have different needs. Oftentimes, however, the needs of account managers are not focused on during implementation. They're more of an afterthought. When that happens, implementation ends, and account management typically ends up saying something like, "Can we create a few check boxes so that we can use this for fulfillment?" Of course you can, but the better approach would have been to involve account management from the start. That doesn't mean you need to implement for account management right away if you have a limited budget or different priorities, but the system could be designed in such a way that, down the line, it will be easier to extend into account management or fulfillment rather than try to retrofit it.

### Product Development

A situation that we see sometimes is that sales makes a forecast, which typically includes some kind of a categorization of the products or services they sell. Sometimes, product development wants to use that for resource or product development planning, but it really is not designed to suit their needs. What they are looking for is not just insight into how they can fulfill the product demands coming down the road; they want to know what customers want in the future—what product improvements or new products they'll be looking for. In many cases, nobody is closer to a client than the sales rep, but there's no formal process for capturing the knowledge that rep has about what a client is asking for and channeling it to the right place, which would be product development. Someone from account management or customer service might be hearing the same kind of feedback from customers, but there's no mechanism to organize that data and say to the product development team, "Here's what we need to focus on."

## THINK BROADLY ABOUT WHO CAN ACCESS YOUR CRM

Not only do you want to think beyond your sales department in terms of how CRM can make an impact, but you also want to think beyond your company in terms of who can access your CRM system. There may be very good business reasons for allowing your customers and your partners (because so many organizations sell through agents, distributors, or outside reps) to access certain areas of your CRM system. Executives are often afraid of this idea. We hear reactions like, "You've got to be kidding? We can't let our customers inside our CRM. That's proprietary stuff. It needs to be secure." They're afraid that partners or customers will gain access to information they shouldn't have. But we can put up restrictions so they only see what you want them to see.

The payoff can be big. Imagine having access to your partners' trove of information about the customers. Companies that sell through partners or agents often lack direct access to their end customer and, therefore, miss out on opportunities to better understand who they are and what their needs are. But if your partners are allowed access to your CRM and use it to store all their customer information, then you can gain a lot of insight into the customer that you didn't have before.

## SIGNS THAT YOU'RE NOT THINKING BROADLY ENOUGH

- You have not thought about or talked to anyone in your company outside of your sales department about how CRM might benefit them. (Think marketing, operations, accounting, legal, product development, etc.)

- You have not thought about how people outside your company might be affected by your CRM or benefit from access to it, including your customers and partners.

- You have not looked at your entire customer life cycle and ways in which CRM might benefit each phase of it.

- You have not taken the time to learn about the wide range of things that CRM can do, beyond just managing sales pipelines and contacts.

## THE BENEFITS OF THE BROAD VIEW

More often than not, by the time a business like ours is called in to implement CRM, decisions have already been made about what the company wants from their CRM. Too often, what drives a CRM implementation is a limited and preconceived idea of what a CRM can do. The most common driver we see is a sale executive who says, "We need a CRM so that we can centralize the data and give it more visibility. We want to know who's doing what and what their pipelines look like."

What we've really tried to do in this chapter is help you see the range and scope of what's possible *before* you make those decisions, so you can make informed choices about what's going to have the greatest impact on your business and create an overall plan based on that. The downside of not thinking broadly is that you can end up with a lot of disruption down the road. For example, say the VP of sales is the sponsor of your CRM project. Because his orientation is all about sales, marketing is not involved, and customer service isn't involved. A company like ours comes in and implements a CRM system, and the VP of Sales thinks he's accomplished something. But then those other departments catch wind of it and start saying, "This is what we need out of the system." Had they been involved from the beginning, their input would already have been taken into account. Plus, you wouldn't have created the kind of culture problems that result when people feel ignored and left out of the process. Accommodating their needs would already be part of your long-term plan, even if they weren't part of the first phase of implementation. We've seen many *many* cases where this was not the approach that companies took, and they paid for it in the long run with a lot of unhappy people in other departments and a lot of time and resources spent retooling and redesigning their CRM systems.

In addition, when you start by thinking broadly about CRM, you have a real opportunity to take a hard look at your business and think about how you can have more effective processes and better communication between individual employees and even whole departments. You can really consider your customer experience and how it might be improved. You have a chance to diagnose problems and see new opportunities for growth.

Many companies put in systems like this, not to reduce headcount but to be able to grow without having to add any more people. Part of being able to do that depends on thinking broadly about questions like, "Where are we really going with this?" and, "How far can we take it in terms of improving our business?" Starting with a broad vision will give you the most payoff. After that, the next step is a bottom-up approach to implementation.

# CHAPTER 5

# TAKE A BOTTOM-UP APPROACH

The purpose of starting off with a broad view is to maximize your potential and create a strategic plan for implementation. Once you have that, the next step is to implement from the bottom-up. The reason why this is so important goes back to many of those "wrong reasons" we talked about in Part I. CRM is never going to be successful unless you get buy-in from the people who will be using it most. As we mentioned in the Introduction, the primary cause of failure for CRM, according to a Forrester Research study, is a lack of user adoption.

Remember, CRM is not a one-size-fits-all solution. It can and should be tailored to your business. How do you do that? You start by understanding not what management wants but rather what the people who are going to be using the system most would like to get out of it. By consulting your main users up front and involving them in the implementation process, you will be driving adoption, even if everyone doesn't end up getting *exactly* what they want in the end. You will also be ensuring that the system is actually helpful to those who will use it most.

## A DAY IN THE LIFE OF YOUR MAIN USER

As we've talked about before, one of the main reasons why CRM fails is because the main users don't find it relevant to what they're doing or they think it's a burden to use, so they just don't use it. We saw this happen when we did an implementation for a large manufacturing company. Initial implementation of CRM often excludes bringing in information from ERP systems that sales reps find extremely valuable, and that's exactly what happened with this company. Their initial implementation was a basic CRM that allowed reps to centralize their accounts and contacts, keep track of their pipeline and activities, and so on. The feedback from the sales reps was basically all the same. They said, "This thing has zero value because I can't go into an account and see what a client's sales history is. If I'm on the phone with the client, I need to know what we quoted them last year. I need to be able to see that they requested a quote two days ago. Without that kind of information, this thing is useless to me." Of course, the needs of sales reps vary by industry, business model, and so on, but this example shows you how important it is that the system is tailored to the needs of its main users. What information do those users need to get their job done?

That's why it's so important, from the outset, to understand what's going to work best for the users and inspire them to *want* to use CRM to improve the way they work by taking an incentive-based approach. You can only do this if you have a good understanding of how your main users do business every day.

In many cases, your main users are going to be your salespeople. Some basic questions you want to be asking are:

- What is your core business?

- How do you sell? (i.e., Face to face? Over the phone? Is there a lot of travel involved?)

- How are salespeople compensated? (i.e., Are they commissioned salespeople? Salaried?)

- How long is a typical sales cycle?

- Is social media used as part of sales practices?

- What are the biggest challenges for salespeople?

The answers to these questions can have a direct effect on how your CRM is designed. For example, if your business sells mostly over the phone, then your salespeople will have different needs than somebody who spends a lot of time in the car and making in-person sales calls. The former would likely benefit from telephony and CRM integration. The latter kind of salespeople could really benefit from a GPS mapping feature that helps them route their visits in the most efficient way.

Once you get a picture of how your main users do business on a daily basis, you want to look at what you can do to improve things for them. This is where you really need to talk to those users and understand, on an emotional level, what is going to help them be happier in their jobs. What will help them be more successful? What will make their lives easier? Once you understand that, you can work backward in terms of what you need to get out of CRM.

Another benefit of having this sort of discussion with users is that it helps bring them on board. Once CRM is implemented, users are going to have to be receptive to new ways of doing things. It's not just going to be business as usual. One of the big ROIs of CRM, as we mentioned before, is that it can really help people be more efficient in the way they work. But that may mean that a sales rep, who may have used the same method of tracking when to follow-up on a call for years and years, now has to be willing to do it a different way—even though his old method was working just fine for him. If you get him involved from the very beginning by asking him how he works and what can help make his job easier or more efficient for him, then he'll be a lot more willing to try a new way. As opposed to simply going to him one day and saying, "Hey, we have this new system. Forget about how you've been doing things all along, even though it has worked just fine for you, and now do it this way instead." How receptive would any of us be to that?

## A DAY IN THE LIFE OF YOUR SECONDARY USERS

As we have made a big effort to point out, a lot of companies don't realize that CRM can extend far beyond the sales team. If you mapped out your customer life cycle in the last chapter, then you should have a pretty good picture of just how many different people and departments touch the customer. Now is a good time to revisit that map, so you can think about who else needs to be consulted before you make decisions on the design of your CRM.

For example, if your business has call center personnel, they may end up using CRM on a regular basis. Just like with your sales team, it's important to get a picture of how they will use it and what features would benefit them the most. You might ask them things like, "What is your biggest priority? Is it getting through more calls in a day or getting higher survey ratings from the customers? What are the biggest barriers to meeting that priority?"

Think about potential users in marketing, sales operations, account management, customer service, and so on. Consider who else might be using this system regularly and make sure to get their input early, rather than after the system has already been implemented.

## TAKE A BOTTOM-UP APPROACH TO DATA

When executives start to understand all that CRM can do, a lot of them get caught up in picturing all the different kinds of data that they will have access to. CFOs, as we talked about in our "wrong reasons" chapter, may focus on all the KPIs. Managers may focus on the insight they can get into their employee's activities. But that kind of thinking typically leads to disgruntled users who resent having managers looking over their shoulder and having to keep up data that doesn't help them do their job. You can avoid this by taking a bottom-up approach to your data.

Just because CRM has the capability to do a lot of things and store a lot of different kinds of data doesn't mean you want to take an "everything and the kitchen sink" approach to your design. Looking at data from the bottom up is going to help you make strategic decisions, ones that are focused on helping your users do their jobs.

Bringing transactional data into CRM can really be beneficial for your users, for example. Being able to see up-to-date accounts receivable information or up-to-date sales, shipping, and invoice information can be really valuable. If a sales rep is going to see a customer, and she knows that customer has an invoice of $10,000 that is 200 days overdue, that's a red flag to the sales rep. She knows something is up with that account and that maybe she shouldn't spend too much time there.

On the other hand, we had a customer once that had us build 20 to 30 fields to profile their accounts. They wanted to know things like the top five competitors for each account, what those competitors' products were, and how much business the account was doing with those competitors. Well, as you might expect, three or four months after implementation, none of that data was up to date because it was just too time-consuming and complicated for salespeople to keep it up. It was just a lot of wasted effort in the end.

Today that company has focused their efforts on keeping just a couple of key fields up to date, especially around opportunities. One of the primary reasons why the company wanted a new CRM in the first place was to get their salespeople to keep their pipelines up to date. For the most part, they have done that. There is very high adoption around these key ingredients, but then there are dozens of fields that hardly anyone, if anyone at all, pays attention to. The client would have been better off starting with the basics for pipeline information and then adding fields strategically as they went along.

You want to look first at data and information that sales reps will find most useful. After that, there still might be areas that you want insight into, which will require sales people to keep the data up to date. If you can't sell it to them as something that's going to help them do their jobs, then you have to come up with strategies and resources that will help them maintain the data you want. Having an admin whose job it is to help sales people keep their data up to date is a great way to accomplish this. (We'll talk more about this topic in our "ongoing investment" chapter in the next section.) That person might print out a spreadsheet, for example, and have sales people check off boxes as an easy way to ensure the data is accurate. That person can also take responsibility for making sure data is kept up to date by reaching out to sales people periodically. If they don't have to take sole responsibility and they are given the right kind of support, most of the time sales reps will be willing to meet you halfway when it comes to keeping up the information that you want.

## ALIGN NEEDS WITH YOUR STRATEGY AND INVESTMENT

Once you understand everyone's needs and wants for CRM, you're going to have to set some priorities. You can't and shouldn't do everything, especially not at first. An executive may have said, "I want to see how many calls per week my sales rep is making. I want to see what his pipeline looks like." Well, that's all well and good, but the sales rep wants to see more information about the customer. Now, accommodating the sales rep by bringing in data from a third party system (such as an ERP, for example) can be more expensive, but if you take into account what we've said about gaining user buy-in to drive adoption, then you really should be prioritizing the needs from the bottom up. In other words, if you invest even $5 in a CRM and get nothing out of it because your sales reps aren't using it, then you shouldn't have wasted that $5 in the first place. If your budget and timeline allows, then you can consider meeting both the executives' and the sales reps' needs all at once, but that will mean a greater investment in terms of both time and costs. But if you have to make choices on what to do first or what to do at all, start with the needs of your users and build from there.

Sometimes, however, you have to deal with the fact that what the users want just isn't feasible. We had a project once where the company did everything right at the outset. They had identified the right stakeholders, had a clear scope, got demos from a CRM vendor, and everything was ready to go. When we got involved, however, the plan started to unfold because in order to make the system work exactly the way their users wanted it to, the project cost was going to be beyond their budget. They had wanted to build in quoting, but their quoting process was far too complex for the CRM to handle without a lot of expensive customization. The company plowed ahead anyway, making compromises to allow for budget along the way, and ended up with something that the sales reps said they couldn't use. They would have been better off going back to their reps and adjusting their priorities and expectations to suit the limits of their budget rather than trying to give them pared-down version of what they wanted and failing. A better strategy could have been to just do a basic CRM implementation, meaning just accounts, contacts, pipeline management, and activity. Their reps did a lot of cross-selling and upselling, and just being able to see what other reps were doing in the same account could still have had enormous value for them. Then, they could have continued to use their old systems for their complex quoting process. But that's not what they did. They didn't go back to align the needs of their reps with the realities of their budget, and today their reps don't use the CRM system at all.

## KEEP AN OPEN MIND, AND THEN
## TAKE A REALISTIC APPROACH

Taking a bottom-up approach means being open-minded at the start, as you go through a kind of discovery and consultation process to find out what different stakeholders truly need and want. A lot of companies want their CRM implementation done quick and cheap, so they come to consultants like us and say, "Just implement the basics" or "Just do whatever you do for other customers." We might ask, "Are you open to looking at other ways of doing it?" and the answer will be, "No, because I just need to get it done." That's a pretty common scenario, but the problem is that it severely limits what you can get out of the project. And it may set you up for failure because your main users won't get what they need. That, as we know, can either lead to a costly retooling of the system or to the system, despite all you invested in it, simply not being used at all. When you first talk to your stakeholders and to the consultant who will be implementing the system for you, it's important to start off with an open mind. That's the surest way to get the best result.

After you've looked at what's possible, you then have to reconcile that with what's practical. If you really want to take this and grow your business, then you are going to need to allocate time and resources to make it happen. But that has to be in line with the realities of your business situation. There are a number of options to consider, including an implementation that unfolds in stages or one that starts with just the basics and builds from there as your budget allows.

Strive for a manageable, viable solution in the initial phase. It should have enough capability to drive user adoption and positive ROI and can be implemented quickly. You will learn a lot from your initial implementation, which will have carry-over benefit to the next phases.

## GETTING EVERYONE ON THE SAME PAGE

The best approach to CRM is to 1) get input from all the different stakeholders; 2) take that input into consideration when setting goals; and then 3) make sure those goals are clearly articulated, defined, and understood by everyone—management as well as users. Doing all this can be a difficult task, but it's also crucially important. If you're contemplating a complex implementation or are having trouble with this kind of bottom-up process, it can be very beneficial to bring in a consultant to help you do an initial study.

If you do the study internally, if the VP of sales comes to the sales team and says, "Hey, we're thinking about implementing a CRM system, and we'd like to understand how you work and what the goals should be," those reps may not be totally up front about what they really think, depending on what the relationship is like. But someone who is an expert will not only know the right questions to ask, but, because he's not the boss, he will be more likely to get real, honest answers from employees about their goals and work habits.

It doesn't have to be an expensive engagement either, but it can pay all kinds of dividends on the back end when you have a system that everyone is on board with and that meets your goals. Management may say things like: "I want my sales reps to be able to see sales to quota," or, "I can't see what the sales reps are doing, so we need a CRM," or, "We want to get quotes more quickly." But if you ask the sales team, who are the main users, they might say, "I can't create quotes any quicker." And if they truly can't, then the whole reason the executive wanted the system in the first place isn't going to pan out. A consultant can come in and talk with both sides to find out what the sticking points are and help figure out if the sides are aligned and aiming for the right goals. That way, when the project gets approved, both management and the users are thrilled about it because they all know what the goals and benefits are going to be.

On the other hand, if a company embarks on a project just to track sales rep activity, what sales rep is going to be excited about that? Not a one. But if you have a project where the focus is going to be on freeing up the reps' time, so they will be able to get out quotes more quickly, spend more time with clients, and ultimately increase revenue and commissions by, say, 15 percent, those reps will be lining up saying, "I want to be part of that project."

Very few companies do this kind of study upfront, and then they really struggle to get the entire team working toward a common goal. As consultants, of course we can implement the basic functionality to track accounts, contacts, and opportunities, but that's not really much of a goal. The goal might be to increase the number of quotes per week from four to six, for example. If defined upfront, everybody can work toward it … management, the users, the consultants implementing your system; everyone can be on the same page.

## KEY QUESTIONS

- Have *all* the key stakeholders within your organization been consulted and provided input on the direction of the CRM?

- How receptive are you to recommendations, and how receptive are you to paying for those recommendations?

- Have you distilled everyone's input down into objectives and priorities that everyone can get on board with?

- Are your objectives in line with what's possible—both in terms of what CRM can do and what you can afford?

- Have you developed a roadmap that documents what you want to accomplish in each phase of this project? Have you shared this with the entire team?

# CHAPTER 6

# IMPLEMENTATION BEST PRACTICES

Even though CRM is not a one-size-fits-all solution, these implementation best practices really do apply across the board. That's because they're about the *process* of implementation, not about the end result, which may look very different or encompass a wide variety of different features and capabilities, depending on the needs of your business.

These best practices have been developed over many years of working on hundreds of CRM implementations. They are a good starting point for any business, regardless of industry, company size, or budget.

## GET *ALL* ROLES INVOLVED—UPFRONT AND ALWAYS

This is really another way of saying to take a bottom-up approach. It's about getting *all* the key roles involved upfront, and not just the executives, and then keeping them involved along the way, as decisions are made, testing is done, and through the various phases of implementation. Too often, sales reps and other key users get overlooked during the implementation phase, and then, after implementation is complete, management dictates to them how they need to use this system and change their behaviors as a result. That's when adoption suffers. From a business perspective, it just doesn't make sense, especially since there are a lot of different ways that you can help ensure sales reps are satisfied to drive adoption.

## FOCUS ON USER PRODUCTIVITY FIRST

This, too, reinforces the bottom-up approach. The best practice is to focus on the needs of your primary users first, which are typically (but not necessarily exclusively) your salespeople. This is a point we've tried to drive home throughout this book. It doesn't mean that the needs of management are unimportant; it's just that they shouldn't be your first priority. This approach, combined with the step above, is the best way to ensure that 1) the system is actually useful to those who will be using it most; and 2) you have buy-in from users so they are willing to use the system, even if it means changing some things about they are used to working.

## START WITH A STREAMLINED, SIMPLE INITIAL DEPLOYMENT

One of the biggest mistakes companies make is to create dozens of fields about an account, opportunity, or contact and then expect salespeople to keep those fields up to date. Well, they never do. Best practice is to start with a very simple segmentation of your accounts. If you need to classify them by prospect or industry, that's fine, but think first about the basic information that will be most useful.

A good rule of thumb is to not put any field or data in the CRM that the users aren't going to understand or keep up to date.

That's particularly important up front, when people are first introduced to the system. If there's too much to learn or wrap their heads around, if it looks like it's going to be a pain from the start, then it can be very hard to alter that first impression, even if you do simplify down the road. So start off simple and implement incrementally. Once you get buy-in and users understand how to use the system, then you can add more complexity as you go along.

A common example of this is sales processes that include too many stages. By stages we mean where the opportunity or prospect falls in your sales process, which could be the qualification stage, the demonstration stage, the trial stage, and so on. Typically, those stages are tied to the probability that the prospect will become a sale. But we've had customers who go beyond the typical stages and say things like, "Once we've got a verbal agreement, I want to know when the contract has been sent. Then I want to know the status of the contract." Sales reps simply don't keep that level of detail up to date. If you want a general idea of where you stand with prospects, keep it to five or six basic stages in the sales process. It's common for executives to want to go into the CRMs and see all kinds of KPIs that show them precisely who the account is and where it is at any given moment, but it's unrealistic to expect salespeople to keep that level of data up to date, especially for an initial launch. It's hard enough just to get them to understand the basics. It would be like expecting them to go from 0 to 100 miles-per-hour in a car in just two seconds. It's impossible to go from nothing to everything without some steps in between. And, as we've seen, many organizations have gross over-expectations of how much time and effort sales people are going to spend updating data.

## PASSIONATE SPONSORSHIP—SOMEONE WHO KNOWS AND USES CRM!

This is an extremely important point, and it can't be underestimated. This is about having *passionate* sponsorship for the project. And not just passionate but *knowledgeable*. The sponsor should be someone who the main users know and respect, somebody who has credibility with the team, like a VP of Sales. It should really be someone who understands the frustrations and challenges of sales and how incredibly tough the job really is.

Though the sponsor doesn't need to be an expert, it should be someone who uses the CRM. The best sponsors are those who really understand the platform and are constantly selling it to the users by saying things like, "Hey this stuff is great! Let me get on my smartphone and show you how I can update the pipeline in two seconds." Or, "Let me show you how I can run a real-time report of all the prospects who haven't been called in two months." Or, "Let me show you how I can look at my tasks list on my phone, and then, if I've got a phone call to make, I just click on it and it dials the number for me." Or, "Let me show you how you can use an app to do a quick voice-to-text translation of your notes on a prospect."

That's the positive way to drive adoption. The negative way is to say, "You people have to use this system and you have to keep this data up to date. Here are all the KPIs we want, and we expect you to do it." Guess which way is more effective? The problem is that 90 percent of the time, we see the negative way, and only 10 percent of the time do we see passionate sponsorship.

## CONSIDER HAVING A TRAINED AND DEDICATED ADMINISTRATOR

Something that every company should consider—especially if they desire a lot of complexity built into their system in terms of things like data classification and segmentation—is investing in what we call a "CRM Administrator" to keep the system up to date. That means a person or people whose job it is to support your main CRM users. That can mean troubleshooting when a user is having a problem, or it can mean helping to keep data up to date. It can mean creating reports on what data is missing and sending a spreadsheet to sales reps so they can quickly update it. Then the admin takes that information and imports it into the CRM, thereby taking responsibility for the accuracy of the company's data.

The basic qualifications for this kind of admin, or what's sometimes referred to as a CRM Coordinator, are as follows: It should be someone close to the business. It should be someone with an aptitude for technical things. Typically it's somebody in sales operations, who has credibility with the sales team, or it's an IT professional with some background in programming.

The other critical thing—and this is where companies often fall down—is it should be someone who has enough time to dedicate to the role. Too often, companies don't allow the person enough time to play their role effectively. They say to someone in their organization, who already has a full-time job, now you're also going to be the CRM coordinator on top of everything else you have to do. If that person isn't going to be accessible to the sales staff and isn't able to take on the responsibility of providing support and maintaining data, then you really don't have an admin at all. (We'll talk more about this subject in chapter seven.)

## HAVE A USER PILOT PROJECT TO TEST THE SYSTEM

A lot of companies skip this step, and it's to their detriment. The main idea is that you want to get a group of key sales people or other users together to try out the system in their day-to-day work life, typically in pilot mode. Doing this is going to give you great feedback on what's working and what's not, as well as some new ideas that can be incorporated before a major roll-out. Even a couple people are enough for this kind of pilot.

In contrast, here's what we run into far too often: a few executive sponsors or somebody from sales operations will work with us on requirements, and they will do the testing. Then the system is rolled out, and the sales people say, "This really isn't what I want."

Or maybe the sales people were involved in the initial requirements and design, but they didn't get to do a formal pilot. Even if you have sales people look at prototypes, once they start using the tool in the real world, they may have a lot more ideas about what it should do or what needs to be changed.

## REPETITIVE TRAINING, IMMEDIATE SUPPORT

Most sales reps aren't thrilled by the idea of sitting in on a half-day or a daylong training. If you get their attention for an hour, you've done well. After that, they're texting or emailing. But if they don't have the right training or don't know where to turn when they have trouble, then adoption is going to suffer.

If you have the kind of admin we talked about earlier, then there will be someone available to help users whenever they need it. For example, we had a client who posted a schedule of admins for the entire sales team to see, and then sales reps could simply pick a time that was convenient for them to show up and get some help. The concept was for training to be driven by the user's schedule, not the other way around. If someone wanted one-on-one training on how to update the CRM from their mobile phone, for example, they could do that whenever they had some free time, rather than having to take a half-day to go to a training class. That kind of immediate support, available when the users need it most, can really help drive adoption.

By repetitive training, we mean you can't expect sales people to sit in on one four-hour training class and learn everything. You can get them started that way, through an introductory web or classroom training, but after that, you need to provide them with ongoing resources. That way, if they have questions or more learning to do in a particular area, they know where to turn, rather than just throwing their hands up and saying, "This is too much trouble."

## REPORT AND DASHBOARD DEVELOPMENT LAST

The executives driving a CRM project often want certain KPIs and a lot of dashboard development. Well, as we've seen, you have to have data in the system, and that data has to be reliable and accurate first, otherwise what's the point of those dashboards? There's nothing wrong with launching without much in the way of reports and dashboards and then evolving those pieces once you get a handle on what data is in the CRM and whether it's reliable and being updated. There are times, however, when a client will become too focused and spend too much time on reports and dashboards and want those things too early. In fact, dashboards and reports can be built really quickly if you know exactly what you're going after. But if you build them too early, before you have a handle on the data they're pulling from, you will end up rebuilding them or not using them at all.

We once built dashboards for a client, for an initial CRM launch, with over 40 graphs on them. We're not sure if anyone even understood it, but that's what the manager in charge insisted they needed. It's better to start off simple and make sure the data you want is being entered accurately and reliably. Only then will your reports and dashboards have meaning.

## ESTABLISH A CONSISTENT MEANING FOR YOUR DATA

Related to the above point is to make sure the data you're collecting means the same thing to everyone who is entering and using it. We had a dashboard training session once with a client where it came to light that various people thought certain terms meant entirely different things. It's not uncommon for operations to view a certain field one way and sales to view it another way. For example, let's say there is a field called "Close Date." Sales may use that field to record the date that they close the sale. Finance may use it to mean the day the business gets booked. Operations may use it as the day implementation starts. It's important to establish a consistent meaning for your data in order for it to be useful.

## LEVERAGE VENDOR RESOURCES

This is perhaps a small point, but big companies like Salesforce are rich in resources—whether it's local user groups, sales engineers, blogs, conferences, seminars, video training on new releases, and so on. It's amazing how often companies are simply unaware of these resources, even if they've had a CRM for some time. Or if they are aware, they don't take advantage of them.

This again goes back to the importance of investing in an admin. If you have all these resources, then someone needs to be given time to research and make use of them.

## PARTNER WITH YOUR PARTNER

What we mean by that is, as an implementation partner, we'll do our best to understand the customer's business, and we'll bring our knowledge and expertise to the table. We have a lot of experience, as a lot of other partners do, but we're never going to understand a customer's business as well as they do. By the same token, they are never going to understand the CRM as well as we do. The best implementations we've seen are with customers who meet us halfway. We do our best to understand their business, and they do their best to understand the CRM.

Customers who make the kind of effort up front that we've been describing end up seeing much more clearly how they can use CRM in their business. At the same time, the better we understand their business, the more recommendations we can make. But some customers are not willing to spend the time, and they are not willing to change the way they do things. They just expect the system to adjust to them—and that sets them up for failure. We use the phrase "CRM is magic" to describe this kind of thinking. It's amazing how many customers have this attitude. But CRM is not magic. It's a tool, and, like with any tool, what you get out it depends a lot on how much you're willing to put in. Partnering with your partner is a key ingredient to success.

## CASE STUDY: LARGE DEPLOYMENT

We worked on a CRM implementation with a large healthcare company that did every one of these best practices, and they did them right. They had a really strong sponsor, who drove the process and took the time to personally get to know the CRM. He was Vice President of Sales Operations, and he had great credibility with the sales executives and the individual sales people.

We worked with that sponsor initially on some designs, but what he did next was bring in a small group of sales people to help create the prototype. We started out by just talking to them, and the sponsor made the process fun. When the sales people came in, it was all about them. "What do you need to be successful?" and, "What would make your day a little easier?" Not: "You need to use this because I want my KPIs." He got them all pumped up about it.

He was a great facilitator because he knew the CRM really well, he knew the business really well, and he met us halfway, helping up to get a better picture of the business and their goals and needs. As a result, we put together some prototypes that really leveraged his knowledge of the company, the experiences of the sales group we talked with, and our knowledge of CRM in the best possible way.

That sponsor also took the time to understand the data that we were migrating to the CRM. During that process, he realized that there was not a consistent meaning across the sales teams for some of their data. He then spent four to six months getting the data straightened out before he launched the pilot, because that's how important it was. That way he was launching with reliable data that everyone understood. We then did a pilot, which was successful, and rolled the system all the way out to several hundred people.

Once the system was rolled out, the sponsor also set the team up for continued success by hiring someone to be the admin or CRM coordinator. And he hired someone with the right aptitude. She had a little bit of background in IT, and she knew the business. He hired her to be in that position full-time so she could be trained and really dedicate her time and attention to making sure the system worked. The salespeople could contact her whenever they needed help, if they had questions or wanted one-on-one training on a certain feature, whatever they needed.

In keeping with our best practices, the initial rollout was simple and streamlined. The sponsor said, "Here are the accounts, here are a couple of fields that you need to keep up to date to keep things segmented, here are your opportunities, and here is a simple sales process that you drop down to keep up the date." Then we created a simple dashboard with a few components that every sales rep used, and that is what they used for their weekly cadence meetings. They didn't continue to do pipeline meetings the old way like some companies we've seen. They adapted their processes—improved them, really—because of the new system. They did their pipeline reviews via Web meetings, during which they all looked at the same dashboards and used them to do their review. By using that standard approach for pipeline review meetings, they got everybody on the same page. Everyone understood what was expected, the meaning of the data, and what had to be kept up to date over the long term.

Over time, we added a lot more to the system. We added custom development to support their operations and to manage their contracts and renewals, among other things. But they started simple and grew the system from there in a smart, targeted way.

The other thing the sponsor did that was so important is he became a continual learner. He developed a relationship with Salesforce.com, which was the vendor they chose, so he understood the resources and could take advantage of them. He would go to conferences to stay current on new offerings and enhancements. And the whole system has been a huge success as a result of all this. His approach resulted in high adoption, more accurate forecasting, and a huge boost in operational efficiencies and sale productivity.

## CASE STUDY: SMALL DEPLOYMENT

We have worked with a lot of financial services companies, such as wealth management firms, that are much smaller organizations but still want a better way to manage clients, to get to know their clients, to track assets under management, and things like that. For example, we worked with a small private equity firm that has done a fabulous job with their CRM. They have only about fifteen users, but even so, they designated a couple of admins to work on CRM, both of whom really stepped up. They were extremely diligent about making sure that everybody understood their data, that it had a common meaning, that there was not an overdevelopment in terms of too many data attributes that were never going to be used. They challenged us to find solutions that fit with how their users worked day-to-day, with how they scheduled meetings, with how they stayed in touch with people. They really pushed us hard by saying, "Wait a minute, we have to come up with better solutions, and we have to look at some third party asset that will make us more efficient." They had the best interest of their users in mind every step of the way as they worked with us, and they took the time to learn the system so they could merge their goals with the system's capabilities in the best possible way. One of the key values that Private Equity firms seek from CRMs is tracking the intertwined relationships between portfolio companies, investors, and referral sources to optimize deal flow. With their focus on ensuring data and data relationships were accurate, they realized those business goals.

## TRAINING BEST PRACTICES

Once your CRM is implemented, the next step is to introduce it to your users and train them so they are up to speed on how to use it effectively. Following are some best practices to keep in mind when you're setting up training for your users.

1) **Training ought to be day-in-the-life oriented versus feature-function oriented**. What do we mean by that? Well, one way to train is to pull up the CRM and show people all its features and how the system has been configured. That's the feature function way, and it's not as effective as making it personal to your users. What salespeople are usually thinking is, "When I get up in the morning and I log in, what do I do?" What you need to do is introduce the system by saying something like, "Step one is you look at your prospect list. Step two is your task list. Step three is how do I manage my existing pipeline?" And so on.

We made the mistake early on of basing training too much around the tool and not enough around the day-in-the-life of the people using it, and it just didn't sink in as well with the users. It should be script based; in other words, it should be based on the sales rep's day-to-day world and how they use the CRM to make that day-to-day world better.

2) **Keep it short and sweet but repetitive**. You might have an initial two- or three-hour training session and then, a month or so later, have another training session to introduce a little bit more. Dumping everything on people at once can be overwhelming, and they just won't retain it all. Getting a handle on the basics first will help drive adoption. Repetition of those basics helps drive retention. Then, when users have a solid base of knowledge, you can introduce them to more sophisticated learning.

3) **Having a trained admin available to users is invaluable**. In our experience, most sales reps, by nature, do not like classroom training. Sitting down for two hours to understand the CRM is just not in line with how they think. But, if they have someone to turn to as questions arise, they're more likely to explore the CRM on their own and learn to make it work. And an admin can check in with them regularly to make sure they are on the right track.

4) **Make sure that admin is well trained and keeps up to date.** That means keeping up with new releases of the CRM and how those can benefit the company. Salesforce, for example, comes out with new releases three times a year, so it's important that someone is keeping on top of those. We worked with a local insurance company once that had appointed two people to be admins, but they simply didn't have the technical aptitude for the job. Years later we went back to show one of their sales leaders a demo, and he was surprised to see that it looked nothing like their CRM. Well, it turned out that they had not updated their user interface in four years. When I talked to one of the admins, she wasn't even aware of the problem. There had been a lot of new features over the years that they could have been taking advantage of, but no one in the company even knew they existed.

# PART III

# FOLLOW-THROUGH

In this section, we will cover how you can make sure you are getting the most out of your CRM system once it has been implemented. This mean taking a long-term view of the resources, time, and attention you will need to put into it to make it work. CRM isn't a static system where, once you've implemented it, you're done. The way to look at CRM is as an ongoing program, not a project with an end date. When you go live, it's just the beginning. There is always more you can do to keep enhancing it and providing more value to your users.

# CHAPTER 7

# ONGOING INVESTMENT

Anything that's worth doing is worth following through on, and CRM is no different. Most people would agree that the way to grow a business is to invest. If you want to grow sales, you have to invest in sales. To grow with your CRM system, to make sure it continues to meet your goals and is giving you a return on your investment, you have to continue to invest in it as well. And that investment doesn't just mean licenses. The ongoing investment you make in CRM doesn't have to be huge, but it is something you need to plan for if you want to ensure your continued success.

A common problem we see is that companies don't allocate resources to maintain the system. In fact, they expect the system to run itself once it's implemented, and that's where they really fall down. You have to think of CRM like other systems you might use. For example, with those manufacturing companies with ERP systems, do they run themselves? Of course they don't. You're constantly changing them based on your business, and it should be the same with CRM. It's true that swapping out a CRM system is a lot easier and less costly than swapping out an ERP system. It's not as big a commitment, but that can often lead people down the wrong path. Because it's not as big a commitment, it's easier to shortchange CRM in terms of long-term planning and allocating ongoing resources. If you had to put in a lot more money and effort upfront, you would be forced to think it through and plan it out. But just because you don't have the burden of costs doesn't mean you shouldn't be planning your long-term follow-through with the same kind of focused attention.

We encourage customers to think through how they are going to govern after they deploy, but in many cases, they just don't get around to doing it. Then, all of a sudden, they go live and their users are screaming, "I have a problem, and I don't even know who to call to get it fixed! Who do I call for training? What do I do when I want a change made to the system?" In such cases, management's only answer is: "I don't know."

To make sure you don't get caught with an "I don't know" as your best and only answer, we're going to talk through how to plan for an effective follow-through. We're going to break this chapter into two parts, because companies typically under-invest in two areas: people and processes.

By "people," we mean investing in a person or persons to be ongoing shepherds or facilitators for the system—the admin or CRM coordinator that we have mentioned before. We will go into more depth about what the right skills are for those people and what roles and responsibilities they should have.

Then we'll talk about "process," by which we mean the model you should be using going forward to manage the ongoing invest-ment, maintenance, and support of the platform. Planning for these two important factors will set you up for long-term success.

## PEOPLE

If you're really going to do it right, you have to invest in a person (or multiple people, if you're a large organization)—what we have been calling an admin or a CRM coordinator—to be the point person for this system. Because if no one is responsible for maintaining it, for making sure it's kept up to date, for making sure that users are getting what they need and know what to do, then these things are bound to fall through the cracks

There are two kinds of problems that companies have when it comes to designating an admin: some don't invest in a person at all (those are the companies that believe the system will magically run itself), and some don't invest enough in that person. We saw the latter scenario when we worked with a healthcare company on their implementation. They had an admin who worked with us on getting the system set up, and she certainly had the intelligence and drive to do a good job in that role. But she simply wasn't given the time to do it. It was a classic case of taking someone who already had a forty-hour a week job, and then on top of it, asking her to be the CRM admin. It just didn't work at all. She didn't have time to learn the system. She didn't have time to sit down with users to understand their needs and then make adjustments to the system based on those needs. She didn't have time to learn how to write reports. She was more than capable, but she barely had time to have a cup of coffee, much less the time to be an effective administrator for their CRM.

Making sure you have someone in place with enough time to dedicate to the task is the first step. The next step is to make sure that person has the right skills for the job.

## The Right Skills for an Admin

The ideal admin does not have to be an IT person; in fact, oftentimes the best ones are not IT people at all. What's more important is that it's someone who is both smart and tech-savvy, someone who is a learner and not afraid of new things. It needs to be somebody who is close to the business and works well with the system's main users. It should also be someone who is able to understand and translate what someone is asking for and apply that to the system. The person should be forward-thinking and not just do what they're told. You want someone who will take the initiative to research new features, bring ideas to users, and be very proactive in terms of what the product can do.

The reason why it doesn't have to be an IT person is that they really don't have to do any programming; it's just point and click, for the most part, if you understand the system well. The reason why it's often better that it's not an IT person is it should be somebody with a few more people skills than your typical IT person has. If you want to drive adoption, you need someone that your users can talk to. The last thing you want is to have your administrator set up a queue to submit questions and issues, so that every time someone sends in a request it goes into the queue and they have to wait for a response. People, especially salespeople who tend to be more people oriented than others, are often frustrated with IT in terms of turnaround time. You want somebody who can get the users what they want quickly and communicate clearly with them, not someone who speaks the language of IT.

The reason why it's so important that it's someone close to the business is because when a user calls and says, "I am struggling with this, can you generate this report for me?" that person has to know the business so well that they can say, "Okay, I know how to filter this report and organize it in a way that's meaningful for this person." Maybe a user is under pressure because he has a sales call in a couple of hours, so he calls the admin and says, "I need a report that shows me all the P&G calls we've had over the last couple weeks." The admin has to know where to go to build the report, the right filters to use, and the right logic to apply in order to do that effectively. The admins have to be the bridge between how the business works and how the system works, so that the capabilities of both sides combine to meet your company's goals.

### An Admin with the Right Sense of Ownership

One common problem that we see is that sometimes internal admins lack a sense of ownership and don't consult with their expert partner when they should. They sometimes make terrible design errors and really horrible decisions. Then, finally, when a partner like us is brought back in, it takes a lot more time to undo and fix what they've done than it would have if they had spent a few hours of consulting time up front so they didn't get off on the wrong tack.

It takes the right kind of attitude to step up and say, "I'm not certain I know what I'm doing here. I'm going to get some outside help." It's very important for your admin to have that kind of open-minded sensibility. And the organization has to back that up by giving the admin the resources he or she needs to be properly trained, so he or she knows the boundaries and can get help from a partner when needed. We worked with an admin in the healthcare field on a very successful implementation. That admin contacted us constantly with questions about design. It wasn't costing her much, just a few short phone calls here and there, but we were able to point her in the right direction every single time.

### ADMIN CASE STUDY

We had a customer who assigned their CRM admin duties to an office assistant. He was great to work with, but he did not have the technical aptitude to say, "Okay, the user wants a list of all prospects in in a certain geography," and make that happen. He couldn't set up the filtering for that to save his life, even though it would require just a few clicks to do it. Months after implementation, he needed to deactivate a user and add a new user, which is about as basic as you can get, and he couldn't figure out how to do it. At the end of the day, having an admin like that means that your users are almost surely not getting all they need to do their job well.

## ADMIN SKILLS CHECKLIST

When finding the right person to be the coordinator for your CRM system, you should look for the following skills:

- Smart and tech-savvy, though not necessarily an IT expert.

- Someone who communicates well with your sales staff or other primary users.

- Someone who understands your business.

- A progressive thinker and continual learner who takes the initiative to learn new features and research updates.

- Someone who is proactive rather than reactive.

- Someone who is not afraid to admit when they don't know something and could use some expert assistance.

## ONGOING SUPPORT OPTIONS FOR COMPANIES LARGE AND SMALL

Large organizations already have established IT governance models, which CRM will typically plug into. In a larger company, a typical situation for providing CRM support is that you have level one support, which might be the help desk or a dedicated admin. Level two support is people who know the application and have more technical expertise. Larger organizations typically have some IT admins to handle really technical things, and that is a good thing because it helps them be fully self-sufficient. Level three is expert technical help. For some of our larger customers, we'll play a level three support role. An issue only comes to us when their internal resources can't solve the problem or accomplish the goal. Then our backup is the vendor, like Salesforce, because if it's a problem in the platform itself, then that's where we have to go to solve it.

The model for smaller customers is going to be significantly different than for larger customers because they typically have smaller budgets for CRM, as well as fewer users to support. A business is probably not going to commit 30 hours a week of someone's time to be an admin if they've got only 15 users. There is nothing wrong with outsourcing the admin role, especially if you don't have the right person on staff to handle it and you don't have the budget to hire someone new. Or you might have someone in the business who is close to the sales staff partner with an outside source to provide this kind of support. It can be a very effective and cost-conscious model to blend internal and external resources to get what you need.

It's when customers say, "I don't need it, and I'm not paying for it because I don't need it," that CRM dies on the vine. This can be a much more pronounced problem for medium and small businesses because they often don't want to pony up the money for ongoing investment. Smaller companies look much more closely at where they're going to spend their money. They might be saying, "I don't want to pay $5,000—$10,000 a year to allocate 20 percent of someone's time to be our CRM admin." Instead, they say, "I'll take my chances." But when they take their chances, they usually get burned.

Whether big or small, what's most important is that you plan for the long term. Who exactly does the work and how can vary depending on what works best for your business.

## PROCESSES

Once you get the right people in place, the next part of planning your follow-through is about asking how those people fit into the project. What is the governance model that you are going to use going forward to manage the ongoing investment, maintenance, and support of your platform?

To get a sense of what we mean by a governance model, ask yourself the following questions:

- How are you going to govern this thing?

- How are you going to handle requests for enhancement?

- How are you going to make decisions on what enhancements you're going to include?

- How are you going to align investments in the platform with your corporate goals?

- How are you going to assign resources to provide support?

## Managing Change

To understand why this is important, consider the following situation. A sales rep calls up your admin and says, "I need to have this check box on my opportunities that indicates it's a high-probability opportunity." What is the admin supposed to do with that request? What often happens is that an admin will create fields and even reports for individual users based on their requests, simply to make them happy. But then, other users have no idea what that new check box should be used for. And those other users may have requests of their own. If you're not careful, you could end up with so many check boxes cluttering the page that it becomes impossible to sort through them all.

This is an example of something that's good for one but is not good for the entire company. A smart, well-trained, and empowered admin will think about the implications of on-demand changes versus planned changes. That admin really needs a process to fall back on for handling change requests, preferably one that's well known by all your users. Because at the end of the day, the system needs to be designed so it suits the needs of the *entire* enterprise as well as the individual users.

When developing such a process, it's often a good idea to think about doing changes in buckets, meaning you say, "Okay, I've heard from various users that they want these ten things. Let's establish priorities on those." A lot of times, users may be asking for essentially the same thing, but they're using different language. One rep might say, "I need a field called 'forecast category.'" Another one might say, "What I really need is a check box to say this should be included in forecast." And then yet another calls and says, "You know what? I really need a text field so I can make a note to myself about whether or not I'm going to forecast this."

The way to handle that is not to make three different changes, each of which makes sense only to the individual user who requested it, even though that may be the easiest thing for the admin to do. Instead, the admin needs to think about what these people are really asking for, which in this case is better forecasting, and figure out one way to solve that problem that meets everyone's needs and then explain it in such a way that everyone understands the change and is on board.

One way that companies handle the ongoing management of their CRM system is to set up a CRM steering committee. These committees typically consist of key users, executive representatives, and the admin. The committee meets periodically to make sure investments and enhancements in the CRM platform are aligned with corporate goals. The CRM admin can bring the feedback he's hearing from users to these meetings, where priorities are then set.

At the same time, the admin does need some latitude to make on-demand changes because, as a sales person, you can't always be waiting for the next meeting to take place in order to get what you need. If the Vice President of Sales calls and says, "I need to know all the meetings we've had with a major client over the last six months," a smart admin says, "You know what? That doesn't have any effect on the data, and it doesn't fundamentally change the system. I'm going to pull together that report right now." That's the beauty of having an admin with knowledge, training, and good judgment. Any governance model should take both planned and on-demand changes into account.

Having a steering committee is something that can work for an organization of any size, because it doesn't take a lot of resources. The frequency with which the committee meets and who is on it can vary depending on the needs of the company. Very large customers will often have an executive steering committee that meets quarterly and focuses more on strategy, and then a CRM committee that meets monthly to talk about and vote on enhancements and that kind of thing. For small or medium-size companies, just having one CRM committee that meets once a month or even quarterly is often enough to stay on track with where the system is going.

### Data Stewardship

Data stewardship is a big part of your ongoing investment, and it is an area that doesn't get highlighted enough. At the end of the day, the success of your system has a lot to do with your data. If your data is not accurate, then your forecast isn't going to be accurate. If your data is not accurate, then your email marketing programs are not going to be accurate. That's why data stewardship needs to be emphasized much more. It's crucial to the success of your system *and* your business. That's why there must be processes in place to ensure that data stewardship is a priority.

A common scenario is when a company starts out with a basic CRM automation, which means entering their contact information, keeping their pipelines up to date, segmenting their contacts by product interest or role or whatever, and that's about it. But then marketing gets involved, and they are just drooling because they can now see all these thousands of contacts categorized by area. That looks to them like a goldmine for their email marketing and target marketing. That is until they realize that none of the data is up to date. Which means it's useless to them.

Salespeople are pretty good at keeping up email addresses and mobile phone numbers, because those are things they need to contact their prospects and clients. But they don't typically have much of an incentive to say, "Okay, I need to segment this client or this contact in a way that suits our mass marketing needs." So the segmentation fields that have been built into the system often end up empty.

This is an area where you really need to have both people and processes in place to ensure you have real, accurate, meaningful data to work with. Since a CRM is only as good as the accuracy and completeness of its data, someone has to take responsibility for it. That usually means your admin or CRM coordinator. It should be a centralized role, so there's just one person responsible who can do things like help the salespeople by extracting their contacts onto a spreadsheet and then spending some time, maybe over lunch with that salesperson, checking off which of their contacts ought to be contacted for a focused new product announcement. The admin can then put that information right into CRM, so it's updated and useful for marketing purposes. That's a lot better process than simply saying to sales reps, "Oh, you need to update all your 500 contacts with the ones who you think ought to get this mailing about our new product." Because maybe they'll do it, and maybe (most likely) they won't.

A lot of companies don't have any sort of standards or governance around their data, and that becomes obvious when you implement a CRM. We feed a lot of ERP data into CRM systems, and that data is typically not a challenge because it's transactional data—an invoice record or payment record, etc.—which is already valid. It's information like the general segmentation of accounts, contacts, and opportunities where we see big problems. And even if you take the time to sort out that data during the implementation phase, it can become out of date and useless really quickly if you don't have an ongoing strategy in place for managing and updating it.

## SETTING STANDARDS FOR YOUR DATA

If you don't have standards or don't have adequate standards for your data, following is a list of questions to help you get started as you create rules to govern it and keep it current.

- What is our process for capturing data?

- Who is responsible for collecting and inputting data?

- Who is responsible for ensuring the right data is being collected?

- Does the data being collected mean the same thing to everyone entering and using it?

## DATA STEWARDSHIP OPTIONS FOR SMALLER BUSINESSES

If you are in a situation where you really can't afford a data stewardship model, it's important to know that going in and understand the results you can expect. If you don't have the resources to dedicate to ensuring you have quality data, then you are not going to be able to use your CRM system for trending and mass marketing. That doesn't mean that your reps can't get a lot of value out of CRM if they take the initiative and keep their own data up to date. But unless you're going to have a data stewardship function, don't expect sales reps to keep tons of data up to date, because you're only setting yourself up to fail.

If you're a small company and don't have the resources to spend, there's nothing wrong with going into this with your eyes wide open and knowing what the limitations are. Understanding your limitations up front can help you make the right decisions. For example, you don't want to put a lot of fields or data elements in the system if you're not going to keep them up to date. But you can still get a lot out of a CRM, like centralized contacts that everyone can access and more efficient processes for your sales reps. Then you can look at adding more down the road as you grow and your budget allows.

## MEASURING YOUR ONGOING SUCCESS

Measurements are important because they are what allow you to say, "Okay, this is working, so let's invest more," or, "It's not working, so let's make improvements." But it's important that you measure your CRM success in the correct way. If you're just looking at CRM as an expense, then you're going to be focused on the expenditures. If you're looking at this as an investment, then you will have a very different perspective on what success looks like. It all comes back to how CRM is being viewed and marketed internally.

If you have done your homework and identified what your goals and objectives are, then it should be easy to track the changes and improvements. The idea would be start with just a couple of measures that you want to focus on. When measuring your long-term ROI, here are some areas your business might focus on to track the benefits:

- Have you increased revenue?

- Have you decreased sales cycle time?

- Is it taking less time and fewer calls to close deals?

- Is your win ratio higher?

- Are you getting to losses faster?

- Are your margins higher?

- Are your costs of sales going down?

- Are you filling your pipelines faster than you used to?

- Are you using fewer resources to close sales?

- Is customer satisfaction higher?

- Are you bringing in more new customers?

These are all business benefits that you want to get out of a CRM. We've given you a rather long list to help you see the possibilities and spur your thinking, but it's a good idea to focus on just a few at first and get a handle on them. Remember, one of the best practices of implementation is to start off with a streamlined and simple deployment. The same advice applies here. What are some key areas you can measure over the first year or two? Pick just two or three and focus there.

It's also crucial to make sure the measurements you pick align with your corporate goals. Maybe your company doesn't have a problem with profitability. Your gross margins are always pretty good, but what you have seen happening over the last few years is revenue growth is flattening out. If that's the case, then your key metric might be boosting revenue. Or, suppose you're in the insurance business. For most insurance companies, getting new customers in the door is they key to success, because once you have them, the majority of them will simply renew their policies year after year. For an insurance agency business, their key metric might be net new customers.

We've done this kind of measuring in our own business. Given the high number of new projects we get sign-off on, we needed some automation around the after-sale. One of the things that we implemented in our CRM environment was an automated workflow to notify our people that, "Hey, we need your help to get this staffed and coordinated." That has nothing to do with sales, it has nothing to do with closing the deal, but it does matter in terms of helping the sales team be more efficient and making sure we deliver on our promise. Our salespeople always had to remember, "Hey, did we staff this project?" Now, we can leverage automation to enable someone else within our company to get the project staffed. We focused there and then and measured our efficiency gains around that process.

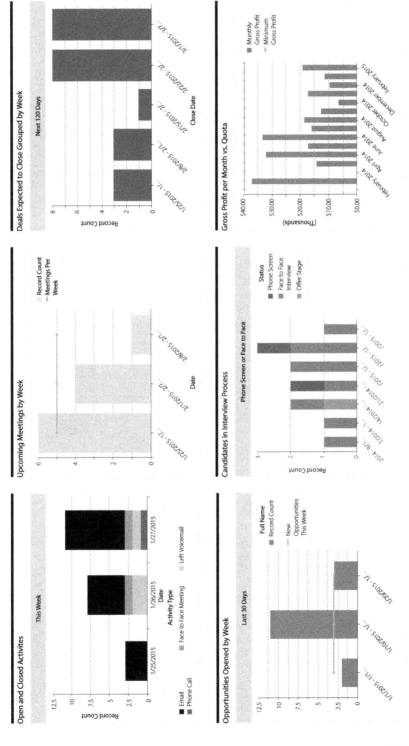

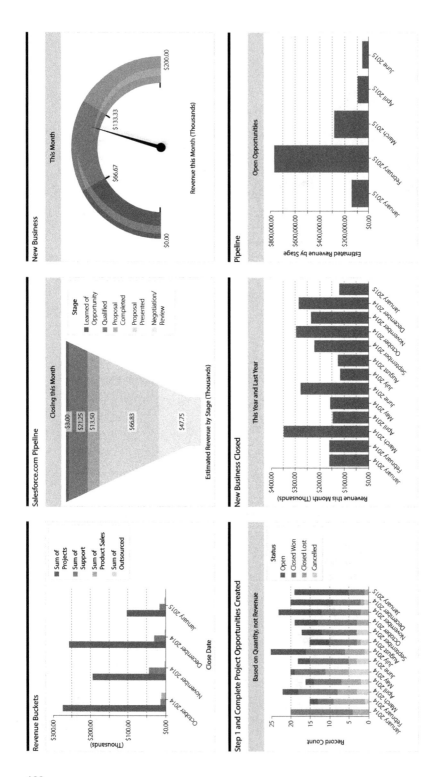

CHAPTER 8

# TAKING IT TO THE NEXT LEVEL

Throughout this book, we have given you steps to take and advice to consider to help you set yourself up for a successful launch of your CRM system. But once you get things going and your people are onboard, there are a lot of things you can do to take CRM, and your business, to the next level. To get you inspired about the possibilities, this chapter talks about just some of the many next-level things that CRM can do. But these are by no means your only options. Don't be afraid to think outside the box, because, for a lot of business, CRM is about a lot more than just managing their contacts and pipeline.

## ENGAGE CUSTOMERS

A lot of the best out-of-the-box ideas when it comes to CRM these days are about direct engagement of your customers. You don't have to have walls between you and your customer anymore. Customer engagement is changing rapidly through the use of technology. CRM can be used to have an ongoing dialog with your customers, get their feedback, and keep them informed about what you're doing. For example, Salesforce offers a platform-specific capability called "Ideas," which we have seen used very effectively. It allows you to develop ideas and products with the input of your customers by presenting them with a new idea and then allowing them to vote on whether or not they like it. They can even offer comments on enhancements or improvements.

Starbucks put this idea into practice by setting up stations in their cafes and offering their customers a chance to give their opinion on what they wanted Starbucks to do. Customers could enter their own ideas or vote on someone else's. It could be new product offerings, service improvements, or whatever came to mind. A common complaint that came out of that experiment was that when customers were driving down the road with their Starbucks coffee, if they hit a bump, coffee would often fly out of the little sipping hole in the top. As a result, Starbucks invented a stopper that you can put in that little hole to plug it, thereby making it splatter free.

Matt doesn't drink coffee, so his contribution to the idea forum was "Sell Diet Coke." When he entered the idea, the system showed him that there were already several other people out there asking for the same thing. So he gave their comments a thumbs-up to give the idea more points. The ideas with the most points would rise to the top and get the most attention.

Some companies are also using their CRM to develop proposals in a different way. In the past, the old model was to write up a proposal in house and then submit it to your customer. In today's world, CRM allows you to develop a proposal *with* your customer, so they can contribute to the process and you can get to the end point together. This makes the customer feel more invested and can also make the process more efficient, rather than the kind of slow back and forth that most of us are used to.

A lot of the more conservative companies are not thinking about things like allowing their customers into their CRM to submit problems or search for solutions. An idea like that doesn't even enter their mind as a possibility, but it can be a highly effective use of your CRM. For example, Activision, which is a company that sells games, has a highly evolved strategy for using CRM to engage their customers. They don't just allow them to submit a complaint form; they have blogs, chats, and customer groups, which are engaging customers and driving product development. Their typical customers are kids who play games all day, and if those kids have a problem with their video game system, they're not going to call an 800 number. They expect a chat session. And they expect, when they are in those chat sessions, that they will be able to provide input on what the product ought to be. The company then uses that feedback to come up with new products or to make improvements on their current offerings.

The traditional, old-school model, where you go do market research, put together some focus groups, and so on still applies in some cases and certain industries. But in a lot of situations, where the customer base is younger, for example, and change happens quickly, that kind of process is just too slow and cumbersome. Now you see blogs, real-time chats, more conversation back and forth between customer and vendor. And CRM can be the platform where a lot of that kind of interaction takes place.

## CUSTOMER SERVICE

Technology has also taken customer service to a new level. Salesforce has been investing in a feature they call "the service cloud," which is a customer service agent offering enhanced service to customers, often in real time. For example, a medical device company has set it up so that if one of their devices has a problem, a notification is automatically sent back to the service center through the Internet and a support ticket is submitted. This can happen before the customer even knows there has been an issue. Not only does that save the customer a lot of time and effort, but it can also be crucially important when it comes to a life-saving device where a malfunction can have serious consequences.

The same company also set up their system so that customer technicians, while on the phone with customers who have called for help, can work together with customers on a picture of the device. Both parties can draw on the picture, so the other one can see what they are talking about. Anyone who has ever been on the phone with someone trying to get some sort of technical support can imagine how this could help the parties communicate better and collaborate on a solution. These are just some of the many ways that technology can be used to communicate with and support customers more effectively than ever before.

## EMPLOYEE ENGAGEMENT

Some of our clients have applied the same tools used in the Starbucks example to the CRM itself. In other words, they have set it up so employees can contribute ideas and vote on enhancements and new ideas. They can submit things like, "I want to be able to do mass emails," or, "I need this kind of report," and others vote on whether that idea is important to them by giving it a thumbs-up or a thumbs-down. It's a great way not only to get employees involved and make sure they have what they need but also to get them on the same page so there is some agreement about what the priorities are when it comes to making changes or adding functions to the system.

There are other simple things you can do to drive adoption, like rewarding a free dinner to the sales rep who enters the most leads. You can even build a dashboard into the system to track the standings and who is in the lead. This idea fits right in with the advice we gave in the Implementation section about taking a bottom-up approach. It gets at what's going to motivate your users to *want* to use this system each and every day, rather than being told they have to use it.

Tools can also be built into your platform to use for ongoing recognition. The system can automatically tout someone's accomplishments by notifying the whole team that "Joe just added 20 new opportunities!" This is a great way to link people together, especially if they're working in different offices and different territories. It can also inspire some healthy competition. Everyone will know what Joe has accomplished and will be thinking about how they can get their own work recognized as well.

Along the same lines, Salesforce has a free app available that a company might have in the lobby, for example. It basically displays graphs, like sales this month. At the bottom is a ticker that scrolls across the bottom, just like you see on ESPN. That ticker might show the ten most recent deals that the company signed or some other accomplishment. People in the company then know, "Hey, if I do something good, it's going to show up here." Practically everybody wants to see their name in lights, so it can be a great way to motivate people and show appreciation for good work.

# TAKE IT STEP BY STEP

Here is a quick summary of the steps to follow to set yourself up for CRM success.

**Step 1: Do Your Research**: This is about having a base of knowledge from which you can make informed decisions. It's absolutely crucial to know the platform, but it's amazing how many people come to consultants like us and say, "Just make it work." You have to ask yourself: Do we understand what the possibilities are? Do we understand the wide range of things that CRM can do? Do we understand what different stakeholders want? Do we understand the potential pitfalls so we can avoid them? (Reading this book in its entirety will have you well on your way to successful completion of this step.)

**Step 2: Get Aligned**: This is about aligning your corporate goals with the goals of CRM. What are your reasons for wanting CRM? Are they reasons that will set you up for success? How are you getting everyone on board and aligned with your goals and vision? You need to define the problems and opportunities first and then design CRM to help provide solutions.

**Step 3: Get Ready**: This is about structuring the initiative. Have you adequately defined your costs and your potential ROI? Who's going to sponsor the project? Who's going to measure the outcomes? Do you have a process in place to make sure users are getting what they want out of it so that adoption is high? What's the right level of investment to make?

**Step 4: Implement**: This is about merging the goals of your business with the capabilities of CRM. Make sure you've thought broadly before you start and that you set your priorities from the bottom up, meaning you address the needs of your main users first. Start off as simply as you can and add complexity as you get a better sense of your needs and as your budget allows.

**Step 5: See It Through**: This is about making sure that you don't just implement it and forget it. Like anything else, CRM needs ongoing monitoring and investment to keep it relevant to your business. That's the best way to maximize your return on investment!

# AFTERWORD

By now, you should have a clear picture of what CRM can mean for your business and how you can start maximizing its potential. More and more people are using CRM these days, and more and more people are getting a lot out of it, too. The estimates for how much companies are getting in return for each dollar invested have been steadily on the rise. As we mentioned in the opening of this book, recent statistics from Nucleus Research tell us that successful companies are getting $8.71 back for every $1 they spend. That's up from $5.60 in 2011, and we expect that number will continue to rise in the coming years.

But you won't be able to maximize the value of a CRM without help. If you really want to be successful, you need to hire an expert to partner with you. People don't implement an ERP system by themselves after all, and a CRM is no different. To get a general sense of whether you're ready to take the next step, take the following quiz and then go to our website at NexGenConsultants.com for a personalized assessment.

Our final piece of advice is this: Don't be afraid. You can be successful. A big return on your CRM investment is well within your reach. The statistics show that you can gain enormous benefits, and we have given you some great guidelines to help you ensure that you're one of the success stories. You now have the information and perspective you need to move forward and see how CRM can have big benefits for your business.

## QUESTIONS TO ASK YOURSELF:
## ARE YOU READY FOR CRM?

Make sure you can answer the following questions:

- Do I really understand what CRM is and the range of possibilities of what it can do?

- Have I defined a desired outcome?

- Have I defined the problems I'm trying to solve?

- Can I commit the *right* internal resources to make it happen?

- Do I have the right mindset?

- What obstacles will I face in gaining adoption?

- Is my culture ready for a CRM?

- Am I sure a CRM will solve my challenges and frustrations?

> **For a personalized assessment and feedback tailored to your business, go to our website at:**
>
> **www.nexgenconsultants.com/are-you-ready?**

# ABOUT NEXGEN CONSULTANTS

NexGen is a Salesforce.com partner committed to helping clients increase profitability through the effective use of CRM.

In October 2007, NexGen was founded by Matt Mountain, who has worked in the IT services market in the greater Cincinnati region for more than twenty years. Matt has sold over $40 Million worth of IT Consulting Services and Software and in doing so, understands the IT Consulting Market from beginning to end. Matt has worked at companies such as LUCRUM, Convergys, and McKinsey & Co. Matt has also been working with CRM systems since 1995, using both Goldmine and Salesforce.com.

Randy Davis joined NexGen in July 2008 as co-owner, bringing twenty-five years of experience in IT services, software, and outsourcing. Randy has worked in technical and business development roles for global information technology companies, such as Cincom, Convergys, and PeopleSoft.

The foundation of NexGen lies in Matt and Randy's IT backgrounds and network of trusted contacts and partners. They create value for their clients by truly listening to their needs and issues and then securing the right resources and recommending the right solution. Their client reference letters directly speak to that approach. During their careers, Matt and Randy built their business based upon the values to which NexGen now stands for. Those values are:

- Exceed the Client's Expectations

- Give more than you expect to receive

- Develop a true Partnership with each client

Using this approach, NexGen Consultants have managed more than 700 CRM implementations since their inception, with an extraordinarily high success rate and quality rate. In fact, they are one of the highest rated implementation partners for Salesforce in terms of customer satisfaction.

For more information, visit our website at:
**www.NexGenConsultants.com**

Printed in the USA
CPSIA information can be obtained
at www.ICGtesting.com
JSHW012037140824
68134JS00033B/3116